MW01101814

a time for
Training Wheels

Family devotions for three to seven year olds

By

Mary-Lynn Chambers

Illustrated by

Jon Smail

Winnipeg MB Canada

KINDRED
PRODUCTIONS

Hillsboro KS USA

a time for Training Wheels
Family Devotions for Children Ages Three to Seven

Canadian Cataloguing in Publication Data

Chambers, Mary-Lynn, 1961 -

  A time for training wheels!

  ISBN: 0-921788-22-3

1. Family - Prayer-books and devotions - English
2. Children - Prayer-books and devotions - English
I. Title.

BV255.C43 1995   249   C95-920197-1

Published simultaneously by Kindred Productions, Winnipeg, MB, R2L 2E5
and Kindred Productions, Hillsboro, KS, 67063

Cover design by Kathy Penner, Winnipeg, MB

Book design by Derksen Printers, Steinbach, MB

Printed in Canada by Derksen Printers, Steinbach, MB

International Standard Book Number: 0-921788-22-3

Dedicated

To the McRae family who provided a platform from which I was free to spread my wings and soar.
To my loving husband Bob whose enthusiasm, involvement and support make our family devotions into memorable events.
To April, Tiffany and Chanelle who are my precious treasures and my inspiration for it in the first place!

Table of Contents

Weekly Devotions for a Year

If you start this in January you will find that the devotionals for special occasions will fall around the date for the celebration.

Making the Most of *a time for Training Wheels*

As children mount their two-wheelers for the first time the eagerness and excitement of success can be seen in their glowing eyes and cocky smiles. But it only takes one spill for them to realize they are going to need some help and support to make this an enjoyable adventure. This is when training wheels become useful.

Family devotions can be like bike riding. God's Word is an adventure waiting to be explored, but for many it can be overwhelming and difficult. *a time for Training Wheels* will give you the support, ideas, direction and creative flair to make family devotions a successful adventure.

Can Family Devotions Happen Successfully?

The unequivocal answer is "yes!" Solomon wrote in Proverbs 22:6 "Train a child in the way he should go, and when he is old he will not turn from it." The challenge is to do this training in a creative way so we keep our children's attention. *a time for Training Wheels* meets this need. For us, family devotional nights are greeted with three cheers as together my husband and I enjoy "training our children in the way they should go."

How Can I Make this Book Work for our Family?

◆ Keep the devotional moving. Don't get stuck on details. Each devotional should range from 10 to 20 minutes.
◆ Adapt the devotional to your setting and to your children's attention span.
◆ Do as much of the devotional as is practical for your children at their stage, needs and interest.
◆ Review each upcoming devotional at least the day before so you are able to prepare without pressure.
◆ Although the lessons can be applied to all, remember, this is a time for the children to learn and enjoy God's Word.

Do I Have to do Them All?

This book can be used in a variety of ways:
◆ Take one series a year, spaced evenly throughout the 12 months. For example, the Fruit of the Spirit series has nine lessons, one of which can be done every six weeks.
◆ Do only the devotionals that are designated for Special Days. These can be done before, on or after the holiday being celebrated.
◆ Use this book on family vacations, allowing each person to choose the one that looks most interesting.
◆ Do 1 devotional a week (there are a total of 52 in *a time for Training Wheels*).

It is my prayer that you will grow as a family and deepen in your love for our God as you begin this great adventure together.

Mary-Lynn Chambers

MAKING MUSIC TO GOD

Materials Needed
- ✔ paper plates
- ✔ stapler
- ✔ macaroni or rice
- ✔ empty tins with plastic snap-on lids
- ✔ construction paper
- ✔ glue
- ✔ markers or crayons

Setting the Stage
In Psalm 92:1-3 we see the Psalmist praising God, making music and proclaiming with musical instruments. We need to learn to do as the Psalmist did. Note: In the upcoming months these new musical instruments can be saved and used during family devotional times to add to the singing experience.

Project
The Homemade Way
- ➤ Take the paper plates and fill them with the dried macaroni using a stapler or glue to seal the two plates together securely. Make sure the staples are side by side so no macaroni escapes. Use the markers to decorate the plates.
- ➤ Fill an empty tin with dried macaroni or rice and cover it with a snap-on plastic lid (coffee tins or potato chip cans work well for this). Secure the lid by taping it in place. Glue the construction paper to the outside of the tin. Using your imaginations decorate the tins so they look great and the children will be eager to use them in the future. Note: Make sure nothing will rub off on the children's hands while they are grasping and shaking the instruments.

The Professional Way
- ➤ Go to a department store, flee market, garage sale or music store as a family.
  While on the drive or walk, discuss how God enjoys music. Talk about favorite songs you could sing to God. Point out how musical instruments can help make singing fun and interesting. Take time to decide what type of instruments you would like to buy. On the drive home try out your new instruments while singing praise songs to God.

Songs
This Little Light of Mine
I Will Make You Fishers of Men
Jesus Loves Me

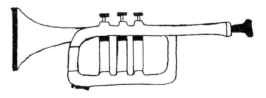

Memory Verse
Ps. 92:1
It is good to praise the LORD and make music to your name, O Most High.

PLEASING GOD IN WHAT WE DO

Materials Needed

✔ 2' x 2' piece of paper (can be the back of a sheet of wrapping paper or a run of computer paper taped together to form a large square) OR one sheet of paper per person
✔ vanilla pudding (chocolate pudding if you do not have any food coloring)
✔ two or three different colors of food coloring
✔ two or three large, shallow containers (for example, a cake pan)
✔ brightly colored markers

Setting The Stage

There are many ways we can please God with our bodies. Ask your children how this can be possible. Direct their answers and help them understand that we can use our mouths to encourage, hands to help, smiles to make sad people feel better, ears to listen to what our parents are saying, etc. Encourage them to think of other ways while you work on this project.

Project

1. Make the vanilla pudding (can be prepared ahead of time). Divide pudding equally and place each part in a separate large, shallow container. Add a different food coloring to each container until the desired color is achieved. The more variety in color the better. Set the containers by the large piece of paper.
2. Have the children dip their hands and feet into the different containers and place them on the paper, leaving behind a colorful hand or foot print. Try to leave space between each print for writing.
3. After all of the prints have been made, ask the children to think of something specific they could do with their hands or feet that would make God happy.

   Examples: Helping mommy by cleaning up my room (hands)
   Coming quickly when I am called (feet)

4. Write the specific actions in brightly colored markers beside the prints, one appropriate action for each hand or foot print.
5. When the pudding is dry, hang the finished product on the fridge or wall as a reminder for the rest of the week of what we can do to please God.

Song

"Head and Shoulders"
(use original tune or "Mary had a Little Lamb")
Head and shoulders, knees and toes, knees and toes, knees and toes
Head and shoulders, knees and toes — (shout) "All For Jesus!"

As you are singing the parts of the body touch each particular part and finish the song by raising your hands and shouting "All for Jesus!"

Prayer

Each person can ask God to help him or her do one of the actions he or she wrote down.

Memory Verse

Proverbs 31:20
She opens her arms to the poor and extends her hands to the needy.

LEARNING TO TALK TO GOD

Materials Needed

✔ five small brown paper bags or dark plastic bags (they need to be nontransparent)
✔ five small items made by God. Examples: piece of fruit, plastic or real flower, Bible, stuffed animal, rock or shell.
✔ children's book on prayer or a storybook where someone had to pray
✔ large piece of paper (2' x 2') (smaller sheets may be taped together)
✔ masking tape
✔ markers or crayons

Setting the Stage

There are many reasons for prayer. We often spend time in prayer only when we have a request. This devotional will help your children appreciate thanking God in prayer. Before you start, you will need to acquire a children's book involving prayer, assemble the mystery bags, each containing one item made by God, and tape the large piece of paper to the wall.

Project

✏️ Read the book on prayer. If you don't have one you can purchase one at any Christian bookstore or check one out of your church library. If neither of these options are available to you, read Matthew 14:23. Discuss the prayer of the person in the story or the content of Jesus' prayer on the mountainside.

✏️ Have the 2' x 2' sheet of paper taped to the wall.   Let each child draw a picture that depicts details from the prayer in the story just read. Encourage the reluctant and inexperienced drawers to try as well. Once the picture is drawn, let the child describe it to you.

✏️ With the filled mystery bags set off to the side have each person sit down. Pass the bags around and let each child feel the outside and then guess what is inside. Once the guessing is done, remove the items and ask the children what all of the items have in common. The answer is that God made them. Point out how we need to thank God for making them and that thanksgiving is part of prayer.

Prayer

Let each person pick one of the items from the bags and say a simple thank you to God for making that item.

Memory Verse

Luke 11:1b
Lord teach us to pray

LEARNING TO OBEY GOD

Materials Needed

✔ video of Noah's Ark (borrow from friend, Christian book store or church library)
✔ box of animal crackers or stuffed or plastic animals (in pairs)
✔ brown construction paper
✔ glue or stapler

Setting The Stage

There are times when it is hard to obey God, but it is very important that we do so. The story of Noah will help your children understand this truth.

Project

Video:

View the video of Noah's Ark or take the time to explain the story to your children. The story is found in Genesis 6-9. The basic details you want to communicate to your children are as follows:

⇨ Noah was a man who loved God. The people outside his family did not love God.

⇨ God was very sad that the other people were so disobedient and mean. He realized that the only way to make the world a nice place to live in was to start all over.

⇨ So God asked Noah to build a big boat. A boat big enough to hold two of every kind of animal as well as his whole family. They were to get inside the boat with the animals while God sent the biggest rain storm ever. Anyone who was not in the boat would die.

⇨ Noah obeyed God, built the boat and filled it with the animals. When that was done he and his family got on the boat. They all lived through the storm. When they were able to get off the boat they were the only ones left on the earth.

⇨ They started over again, but first they took time to thank God by bowing and praying. God answered by sending a rainbow. The rainbow was his promise that he would never send such a big rain storm again.

Ark:

Cut the brown construction paper in the shape of a boat and then cut a second piece the same shape and size. Glue the two pieces together at the sides and bottom leaving the top of the boat open. While the glue is drying open the box of animal crackers, empty the contents and look for matching pairs. Once the pairs have been found, take one of each kind and place them inside your glued boat. If you don't have animal crackers, set stuffed animals around the boat.

Discussion:

Discuss why it would have been hard for Noah to obey God. Here are some ideas:

⇨ There had never been any rain up to that point so Noah didn't even understand the concept of a flood.

⇨ The other people around him made fun of him for making a boat so big and for obeying God.

⇨ Noah must have wondered whether the boat was going to work and how he was going to get everyone on the boat.

Song

"Trust and Obey"
(use the original tune)
Trust and obey, for there is no other way to be happy in Jesus, but to trust and obey.

Prayer

Pray about one area in which you have a hard time obeying. Example: Cleaning your room, coming when you are called, talking kindly to your brother or sister.

Memory Verse

Ephesians 6:1
Children, obey your parents in the Lord, for this is right.

LEARNING TO LISTEN TO GOD

Materials Needed
- ✔ timer
- ✔ tape of a religious children's song

Setting The Stage
No matter how old you are in the faith it is hard to learn to listen to God. This devotional will help your children understand what you mean when you say, "Listen to what God is saying".

Project
Game:
- ☞ Take a regular kitchen timer or another household item or toy that would make a similar soft sound.
- ☞ Have the children leave the room.
- ☞ Turn the timer on and hide it somewhere in the room.
- ☞ Have the children come back into the room and listen very carefully until they detect the location of the timer and find it.
- ☞ Play the game over and over giving each child a chance to find the timer.

Questions and Principles:

Question: How hard did you have to listen to be able to hear the ticking sound?
Principle: You have to stop and listen intently to hear what God is trying to say to you.

Question: Through whom does God speak to you?
Principle: God can speak to you through the Bible, through older, wiser people (like your parents) or through people who really know about the Bible (like the pastor or a Sunday school teacher).

Question: In your life whom does God use to speak to you?
Principle: Learn to know the people whom God uses (therefore name specific names).

Question: In your life what does God use to speak to you?
Principle: Learn the tools that God uses (like music, story tapes, videos, the Bible).

Practice:
Play a song from a children's tape and ask them what is the message of the song. You will want to listen to the song beforehand to make sure that it is a clear, easily understood message.

Prayer
Ask God to help you learn to listen to his voice as he speaks to you in a variety of ways this coming week.

LOVE (VALENTINE'S DAY)

Materials Needed
- ✔ scissors
- ✔ three different colors of construction paper or enough colors so each child has one color
- ✔ chocolate hearts
- ✔ white paper
- ✔ pen
- ✔ bowl

Setting The Stage
Together you will be reminded that learning to act in love, even when it is not easy, is important because of the end result.

Project
Ahead of time:

Cut the letters L-O-V-E from the different colors of construction paper. Pile all the letters together in the center of the floor and sit around the pile.

Now:

First, let the children sort the letters so they have four piles with the same letter in each pile. Then have them color coordinate the letters so they have three piles (or one pile for each color), each pile having enough letters to spell out the word love. If the children still cannot spell, do a sample pile for them by taking the letters from one pile and spelling out the word LOVE. Have them do the same with their own pile. This part of the activity can be made into a game by seeing who can separate the letters by colors or words the fastest or who can spell out the word LOVE without any help.

Ahead of Time:
- ❤ Hide the chocolate hearts around the room (Hint: If you put out more than 10 you might find it helpful to write down the hiding spot or it could be months before all the hearts are found).
- ❤ Explain to them how we celebrate love on Valentine's day by doing something special for the people we love. The hunt is something special you want to do for them. Establish the boundaries of where the hunt is to take place and how many hearts they need to find, then let them go at it.

Now:

While they are enjoying their newfound hearts, sit down and talk about how some of the hearts were hard to find. Point out how hard it was for them to do a certain part of the first activity (whether it was trying to spell the word LOVE quickly or just simply separating the letters by color). Allow this to lead into a discussion of how some aspects of loving are very hard to do. Allow your children to come up with a few examples from your own family life.

Ahead of time:

Write out the following situations on a sheet of paper leaving space between each one. Cut the situations into strips, fold them in half and place them into a bowl. Note: The following situations can easily have an adult play the role of one of the children if two children are not available.

- ❤ Child #1 is mean and speaks unkindly to Child #2; Child #1 pushes Child #2 down. Child #2 doesn't get angry but speaks kindly back to Child #1 and shows Child #1 love and forgiveness.
- ❤ Child #1 is playing and hurts himself/herself. Child #2 sees Child #1 crying and hugs and kisses him or her.
- ❤ Child #1 has a job to do and Child #2 helps with the job without being asked (for example: picking up toys).
- ❤ Child #1 is given a treat and he/she shares the treat with Child #2 without being asked .

Now:

Bring out the bowl and let the children take turns choosing a slip of paper. Read the situation to them and help them understand the role they are to play. Let them act it out. Continue until all the situations have been acted.

- ❤ Using the previous situations discuss how different it can be to always show love.
- ❤ Have each child choose one way they are going to show love this week.
- ❤ Tape the letters L-O-V-E on the fridge allowing the children to choose their favorite color out of the three or more choices. Use this as a reminder all week.

Prayer

Have each child ask God for help to show love in the way he or she has chosen in the upcoming week.

Song

"Jesus Loves Me"
(use original tune)

Jesus loves me! this I know, For the Bible tells me so; Little ones to Him belong, They are weak, but He is strong. Yes, Jesus loves me! Yes, Jesus loves me! Yes, Jesus loves me! The Bible tell me so.

Materials Needed
- ✔ magazines
- ✔ six different colors of construction paper
- ✔ scissors
- ✔ glue
- ✔ ball

Setting The Stage
Throughout the devotional remind your children that real joy comes from doing things that make God happy.

Project
1. Sing a song about Joy (for example: I have the joy, joy, joy down in the depths of my heart — WHERE? down in the depths of my heart — WHERE? down in the depths of my heart. I have the joy, joy, joy, joy down in the depths of my heart — WHERE? Down in the depths of my heart to stay.) Note: If you don't know this tune, it can be sung as a chant.

2. Talk about the different times you feel real joy. Remind them that real joy comes from doing the things that make God happy. Examples: sharing, helping, showing kindness.

3. Use the magazines to find six pictures of people doing something that seems to give them real joy. Cut out the pictures and glue them onto the six different colored sheets of construction paper, one picture on each sheet of paper.

4. Take the six sheets of paper and lay them face down in the pattern diagrammed below. Make sure no one knows which picture is in which spot.

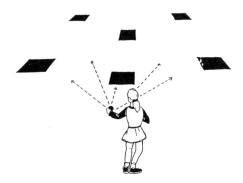

5. Have the child stand behind a line and toss the ball at the squares. Whichever paper the ball lands on is the paper the child may take as his or her own. Have the child show the picture to everyone else. Explain why the person in this picture seems to have real joy. Help the child include the perspective that the person could be doing something that makes God happy.

Prayer
Each person should choose one picture and for the coming week should try to do what is being shown in the picture. Ask God for help in doing what your chosen picture demonstrates.

Song
"I Have The Joy"
(as sung at the beginning of the devotional)

PEACE

Materials Needed

- ✔ pots, pans and large spoons
- ✔ sturdy toys
- ✔ pillows
- ✔ loud food (like chips)
- ✔ television or stereo

- ✔ 8 1/2" x 11" white plain paper
- ✔ glue
- ✔ blue and black construction paper
- ✔ crayons
- ✔ scissors

Setting The Stage

Peace is a quiet calm during which we can know God better. The goal of this lesson is to teach your children what is and isn't peace and how, during these times of peace, you can talk to God and learn more about God.

Project

1. Set up a noisy section on one side of the room. This section will have four stations, each with a number so that the order is understood by all.

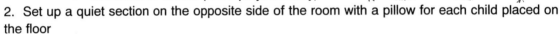

      1 - pots, pans and spoons.
      2 - loud food
      3 - toys (over which to fight)
      4 - television or stereo (to be played loudly)

2. Set up a quiet section on the opposite side of the room with a pillow for each child placed on the floor

3. Start at station number one. Call out GO! and have them do the activity as loudly as possible until you call STOP! When you call Stop! they are to run to the pillows and lie perfectly still and quiet until you call GO! again at which time they will run to the second noisy station and do the activity there. Continue alternating until all sections are visited at least once. Keep this pattern going for about five minutes.

4. Stop the game and have them sit on their pillows. Explain to them how difficult it is to think about anything, especially God, when we are being so noisy. Explain how precious peace is because then we can stop and talk to God.

5. Go to the table and work together on pictures that demonstrate times of peace, times when we can be quiet and be with God. While working on this part of the project discuss how they can talk to God during these peaceful times. You can do one or all of the following depending on the child's interest:

- ➥ Snowfall - Fold white paper in half again and again until it is as small as possible. Cut off the corners. Open and see a snow flake. Glue this snow flake onto a blue sheet of construction paper.
- ➥ Night Time - Take a pointed object (pen) and poke lots of holes into the black sheet. Hold it up to the light and see stars shining at night.
- ➥ Being Loved - Draw and color a picture of a parent giving a child a hug.
- ➥ Bed Time - Draw and color a picture of a child praying before bedtime.

Prayer

Pray for times of peace during which you can learn to talk to God.

Memory Verse

Psalm 34:14b
Seek peace and pursue it.

PATIENCE

Materials Needed

✔ one white sheet of paper
✔ many different colored crayons including black
✔ dull kitchen knife

Caramel Corn

✔ 1/2 cup margarine	✔ 1/2 teaspoon salt	Preheat oven
✔ 1 cup brown sugar	✔ 1/4 teaspoon baking soda	Bake at 300° F for
✔ 1/4 cup corn syrup	✔ 1/2 teaspoon vanilla	20 minutes
✔ 3 quarts popped corn (3/4 cup kernels)		

Place popped corn on an ungreased cookie sheet. In a saucepan melt butter, stir in brown sugar, corn syrup and salt. Bring to a boil while stirring constantly. Lower heat and allow it to simmer for five minutes stirring constantly to make sure it does not burn on the bottom. Remove pot from the heat and stir in the soda and vanilla. Gradually pour caramel over the popped corn and mix well so every piece has been touched. Bake uncovered for 20 minutes at 300° F. Remove from the oven at five minute intervals to stir. At the end of 20 minutes remove a piece from the oven and allow it to cool. If the caramel corn is crunchy, it is done. If it is chewy, allow it to bake a bit longer. Allow it to cool for five minutes, then enjoy!!

Setting The Stage

Help your children understand that having patience means you are willing to take the time to get the desired result and that if you are impatient and rush, the result is often disappointing. The following three activities will show them that exercising patience is usually worth while in the end.

Project

Caramel Corn

Following the recipe, make the Caramel Corn. While making the Caramel Corn spend time talking about how good and crunchy it will be at the end so it is worth the wait. Also, talk about how this is true in other areas of your life. Examples: making your bed, playing a game, talking to people.

> Patience is needed when making Caramel Corn because if it is eaten too soon it is chewy and will stick to your teeth.

Stop and Go

While the Caramel Corn is baking, play the game Stop and Go. The adult stands at one end of the room, turned away from the rest of the family. The family is lined up side by side at the other end. When the adult says, "Go!" they move as quickly as possible towards the adult. When the adult says, "Stop!" they must stop immediately because as the adult finishes calling out stop, he or she will quickly turn around to see who is still moving. Whoever is caught moving must go back to the starting position. It will be advantageous in helping your child understand the principle if you catch them at least once and send them back. Play the game several times helping them understand the role of patience in winning the game.

> Patience is needed in playing this game because the faster you are moving the harder it is to stop and the easier it is to be caught. The person who is the most patient will probably be the one to get to the adult first without being sent back and therefore wins the game.

Love is Patient

While eating the caramel corn have everybody sit around a table with one sheet of white paper in the center. Everyone is to take a different color of crayon (except black) and color the sheet. The object is to use many different colors to make little sections of all different sizes. Once the sheet is covered in color, color the entire sheet again in black trying to cover the color beneath as much as possible. Take the dull kitchen knife (you will be removing the black and revealing the bright colors below) and scratch out the letters that make up the memory verse for the week, "Love is Patient." Say it over and over together until everyone can say it, then hang the verse in a visible place (like the fridge) for the upcoming week.

> Patience is needed to achieve the beautiful end result. Point out how it took a while to make this sheet with the Bible verse on it, but also how it was worth being patient and working on it until it was done.

Prayer

Ask the question, "When are you most impatient?" When all have given their answers, use the answers as a spring board for prayer time. Ask God for patience during those times when we are so easily impatient.

Memory Verse

I Corinthians 13:4a
Love is patient

Materials Needed

✔ ball
✔ puppet theater or table with blanket
✔ five different puppets (dolls or stuffed animals)
✔ small object (pencil, small book or block)
✔ markers or crayons
✔ blank sheets of paper taped together to form a 2' x 2' sheet of paper.

Setting the Stage

Through this puppet show you will have the opportunity to show your children that kindness is a special way of saying " I love you and God does too."

Project

Ball Toss

Everyone sits in a circle on the floor. An adult starts by holding the ball and sharing one act of kindness he or she did this week. The adult passes or rolls the ball to another person in the circle; whoever receives the ball must share an act of kindness he or she did this week. The game continues until everyone has had a chance to share at least one act of kindness.

Play

If you do not have a natural setting for a puppet show, cover the kitchen table with a blanket so the blanket reaches the floor on the side of the viewers. The adult can work from behind the table so they, the puppets and the script can not be seen. Put on the following show improvising wherever necessary. Your show will be a little smoother if you assign a name to each puppet or stuffed animal before the show begins so you know which one to grab as you are changing roles.

A Day Of Kindness

Characters: Mommy, Child, Cindy, Sam, Joe (represented by puppets, dolls or stuffed animals)

Scene I

Mommy: (to child) Today I want you to try to make your whole day a day of kindness.
Child: How can I do that?
Mommy: When you are at school or playing with your friends and you see a chance to be kind, stop and do what is kind...that will make it a day of kindness. (hug good-bye)
Child: Okay, Mommy, I'll see you later. (Mommy waves good-bye and child leaves. Mother drops down behind the scene.)

Scene II

(Cindy is walking ahead of the child as child, returning to the scene, tries to catch up to Cindy who has a small object [pencil, small book or block] in her hand.)
Child: (speaking to herself) Hey, there's Cindy. I wonder if I can catch up to her.(She acts like she is running and panting and catches up to her friend Cindy) Hi! Cindy. May I walk with you?
Cindy: (turns to see who it is and drops small object from her hand) Oh no!!
Child: (bends down and picks up small object) Here, let me pick this up for you.
Cindy: Thanks, that is nice of you.

Child: (Turns to viewers and says) Wow, I just did an act of kindness!!
             (both friends walk off the scene together and drop down behind the table)

Scene III
(Child out playing in the playground - Sam is sitting off to the edge of the scene by himself)
Child: Boy, it sure is fun playing at the playground. Hey , who is that sitting over there all by himself? I have never seen him before. (Looks over at Sam) I think I'll go over and say hi. (child moves over to Sam)
Child: (to Sam) Hi, are you new here?
Sam: Yes, I just moved here and this is my first day at the playground.
Child: Well, how come you're not playing? Hey, what is your name?
Sam: My name is Sam and I don't have anyone to play with so I am just sitting here by myself.
Child: Well, you don't have to do that any longer...why don't you come over and play a game of tag with me.
Sam: (gets up and joins child) You bet! I would love that. Hey, thanks for being my friend and being so nice to me.
Child: I am just showing kindness...No problem at all!

Scene IV
(Eating lunch at school)
Child: (walking with Joe to the lunchroom) Hey, Joe, I am so hungry I can't wait to see what my mom sent for lunch today.
Joe: (looking sad) I don't have to look, I already know. My mom told me that she had to go shopping today and that she had nothing left in the house so I only have half of a sandwich in my bag, and I am really hungry too.
Child: No problem. My mom always sends tons of food and I don't mind sharing some.
Joe: Hey, that's great. Let's go eat.

Scene V
(Child running into the house to see Mommy)
Child: Mom, Mom, guess what? I had a day of kindness just like you wanted me to have.
Mommy: (hugs child) Tell me all about it.
Child: Well, I helped Cindy pick up something she dropped and I made friends with a new boy and I shared my lunch with Joe.
Mommy: Wow! You did have a day of kindness and I'm so pleased (gives another big hug).

Children's Drawings
Tape the large sheet of paper to a free spot on the wall. Make sure the sheet is easily accessible and at the children's eye level. Give each child a section and let them go to work drawing a picture that demonstrates an act of kindness. Note: The puppet show can give them some ideas. When they are done with their drawings, let the children describe what they have drawn. If the children are too young to do a complete drawing on their own, you may sketch a scene and let them color it, explaining to you what is happening.

Prayer
Pray together that each day in the upcoming week will be filled with kindness.

GOODNESS

Materials Needed

✔ one sheet of green construction paper
✔ one sheet of red construction paper
✔ eight small bowls (nontransparent)
✔ tea towels
✔ pieces of paper
✔ pen
✔ scissors
✔ three good-tasting things to eat (small candies, cut up fruit, dried cereal)
✔ three not-so-good-tasting things to eat (coffee grounds, salt, chopped onions)

Setting the Stage

It's important for the whole family to learn to identify what goodness is so we can do it for others. Doing "goodness" means you do a good act that is not naturally easy to do but needs to be done with God's help.

Project

Ahead of time:

Fill the six bowls, three of the bowls with good-tasting food and three of the bowls with not-so- good-tasting food. Then cut six circles, three out of the green sheet and three out of the red sheet.

Now:

Place the bowls in a row on the table. Give the children the red and green circles and have them place the circles in the appropriate places. A green circle means the food is good-tasting and a red circle means the food is not-so-good-tasting. Let them take a little taste of the food if they want to confirm their choices.

Next:

Have them close their eyes. Switch the order of the bowls and cover them with a tea towel. Have the children open their eyes and again try to place the circles in the appropriate spots, but this time it is a guessing game. See how many they get right. Let them play this game several times.

Lesson:

Point out to the children that it is much easier to identify what is good when the tea towel is off than when the tea towel is covering the dishes. Use this to illustrate that sometimes it is easy to see what is the good thing to do and sometimes it is hard.

Ahead of time:

Take the plain sheet of paper and cut the paper into strips. On each strip of paper write out the following good and not-so-good actions leaving out the word in the brackets.

➥ You have a bag of candies and your sister would like to try one so you let her have a few. (green)
➥ Your friend yells at you while you are playing so you tell him that it is time to go home. (red)
➥ You are playing with a bunch of kids; one gets hurt and starts to cry. Everyone is looking at him cry. You go and get your favorite stuffed animal letting him hug it until he stops crying. (green)

➡◆ You have been told to clean up your room. You go to your room and clean it up as fast as you can by pushing all the toys under your bed. (red)

➡◆ You know of someone who is sick. You make a card for him or her and give it to the person to help them feel better. (green)

Bring out the two empty bowls and the strips of paper with the situations written on them. Place one of the green circles in front of one of the bowls and one of the red circles in front of the other empty bowl.

Now:

Explain to them that you are about to read a situation and they are to place the slip of paper in the green bowl if it is a good act and in the red bowl if it is a not-so-good act. As you read each slip, let the children take turns deciding into which bowl the paper should go. Some of the situations are harder to decide and may need to be discussed.

Lesson:

During the discussion remind them of the previous activity where when the tea towel covered the bowls it was harder to determine what was good and how this is also true in real life.

Song

"God is So Good"
(original tune or chanting with a catchy beat)
God is so good, God is so good, God is so good, He's so good to me.

Prayer

Ask God to help each of us find the opportunities to show goodness to other people.

FAITHFULNESS

Materials Needed
- ✔ dolls (or stuffed animals)
- ✔ large bowl (or empty trash can)
- ✔ plastic food (or blocks)
- ✔ one blank sheet of paper
  for each person (or coloring book)
- ✔ crayons or markers
- ✔ pen

Setting the Stage
Being faithful means we are diligent in doing an assigned task and are not easily distracted.

Project
Game: Set up the game following the diagram below.

	doll		
doll	bowl	distracter	feeder
	doll		

- ☞ The object of the game is for the feeder to get the plastic food into the bowl so the hungry dolls can eat their dinner.
- ☞ The feeder must stay behind the imaginary line while trying to toss the food into the bowl.
- ☞ While the feeder is tossing the food, the distracter lies on his/her back and waves his/her arms and legs in the air to try and stop the feeder from doing his/her job.
- ☞ Let each person have a chance at being both the feeder and the distracter.
- ☞ At the end of the game help the children understand how important it is for the feeder to be 'faithful' in doing his/her job; also how hard it is to do the job when someone is distracting you.

Drawing:
Sit down and share about some jobs that each one has to be faithful at doing. After a list has been made let each person choose one job to draw and color on a sheet of paper. Spend the next 5-10 minutes drawing and coloring. (Note: Another option is to go through a coloring book and rip out sheets of paper that have pictures of children or animals doing a job. Allow them to color and discuss the job being done.)

Discussion:
When the drawings are complete, discuss each picture deciding which things could easily distract or keep you from doing the job.

Prayer
Have the children create their own "prayer song" to God about being faithful in their chosen job. They can create their own tune and words and talk to God in this creative way.

GENTLENESS

Materials Needed
✔ deck of cards
✔ raw eggs (or water balloons)

Setting the Stage
We need to learn to be gentle with people and things. Through the activities of this devotional your children will receive a better understanding of gentleness.

Project
1. Together create a song about gentleness. If the children are old enough let them make up their own words. If the children are too young to do this, use the following words to the tune of "Row, Row, Row Your Boat."

> We need gentleness, we need it every day
> The way we walk, the way we talk and
> the way we play.

Practice the song together. Then get out your musical instruments (see Section One Making Music to God) and parade around the house singing your song on gentleness while playing your instruments.

2. Take the deck of cards and each take a turn adding a card to make a card house. The adult will have to start the process (see diagram). Constantly point out how gentleness is needed to build the house. Note: You may want to practice building one on your own first so you have the concept of how it works.

3. To continue the understanding of the principle of gentleness, move outside and have a raw egg or water balloon toss. Have a pair start by facing one another, standing close together. They will gently pass the egg or balloon from hand to hand. Keep emphasizing the need for gentleness. Slowly move them apart, continuing to toss the egg or balloon back and forth until it breaks. (Warn the child before hand that it could get messy. You may want them to wear their raincoats for this activity.)

4. Talk about how important gentleness was while doing the activities. Discuss how we need to also be gentle with people in the way we talk to them and treat them.

Prayer
Ask God for the ability to be gentle all the time.

Song
Sing your new gentleness song again using your musical instruments.

SELF-CONTROL

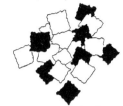

Materials Needed

✔ book or video tape where a character has little self-control (yells a lot, etc.)
✔ plastic farm set (or some stuffed animals)
✔ different colors of construction paper
✔ glue
✔ pencil

Setting the Stage

Let your family know that we all need self-control. With God's help we need to refrain from doing things we should not be doing.

Project

⊃ Choose a book to read or short video to watch where a character continually shows no self-control.

Every time the character shows no self-control have everyone yell , "No self-control!!"

⊃ Bring out a plastic farm play set. If you don't have one you can get the same results with different stuffed animals.

Have the children role play with the animals. No script is needed. Tell them they are to let the animals show no self-control. Examples: Pig eats all the food so that no one has any or sheep wanders off or cow gets angry when it has to be milked. When they are finished role playing explain to them how this is not a happy farm because the animals are not showing self-control.

Let them play with the farm again, this time showing self-control. Show how well the farm works, how everyone gets something and is happy when they all show self-control.

⊃ Rip three - four different colored sheets of construction paper into little pieces and place them into a bowl.

Let each child have a sheet of construction paper. For each one, draw the shape of the animal he/she used during the farm play time. Cover the inside shape of the animal with glue and let each child pick out the different colored ripped pieces of construction paper to fill in this shape. While the glue is drying, challenge each child to learn self-control as their animal did on the farm.

⊃ Sit together in a circle.

Share with one another one area in which you want to learn more self-control.

Examples: Not crying when you are asked to clean up your room.
              Not complaining when you have to eat something you don't like.
              Not getting angry when someone isn't playing the way you want them to play.

Prayer

Pray for the area where you need the most self-control.

Memory Verse

I Thessalonians 5:8b
let us be self-controlled

CREATION

Materials Needed
- ✔ one white poster board
- ✔ multicolored food pieces (M & M's, jube jubes or colored pasta)
- ✔ glue
- ✔ animal crackers (optional)
- ✔ children's Bible (optional)

Setting the Stage
God has made our world a beautiful one, but sin can mess up God's creation. We need to learn to take care of God's world and thank him for the beauty.

Project
Together you are going to create a picture of the Garden of Eden. This picture will be made with small pieces of colored food. You will want to cut the jube jubes so they are more easily glued to the piece of poster board. It will make things easier if you sketch the scene and then assign each person to an area or item on which to work.

Suggestions for the food:

green...	leaves and grass
red...	fruit on the trees
brown...	tree trunk
yellow...	the sun

The animals can be animal crackers or you can design some using the colored food pieces.

While you are gluing the picture in place you can share with your children the story of the Garden of Eden. You may do this from a children's Bible or by retelling the facts in your own words. If you choose to do the latter, the following details should be included in your story.

These details come from Genesis 1-3.
- ➤ The world was created in seven days (ask the children what it was that God created).
- ➤ The Garden of Eden was perfect. There was no pain, no crying and no sadness.
- ➤ God walked with Adam and Eve in the Garden.
- ➤ There was only one rule. Adam and Eve were not to eat from the Tree of the Knowledge of Good and Evil.
- ➤ One day Satan took the form of a snake and came to Eve telling her she would become like God if she ate the fruit from the Tree of the Knowledge of Good and Evil.
- ➤ Both Adam and Eve ate the fruit. This was the first sin.
- ➤ Because they sinned they could no longer stay in the Garden of Eden.

When you are finished the picture and story, point out to the children how beautiful their picture of the Garden of Eden looks .

↷ Take the time to discuss the beautiful parts of creation we see in our world.

↷ Ask them to mention what makes our world less than beautiful.

↷ Help them see that it is sin that makes our world a mess.

Song

"God made the _____"

(use the tune of "God is So Good" or a chant style with a catchy beat)

God made the ____, God made the ____, God made the ____ He's so good to us.

Allow each child to call out a part of creation that they love when you come to the blanks in the song. This can be sung over and over until you have exhausted their choices.

Prayer

Thank God for his beautiful creation. Ask God to help you keep it beautiful.   Older children can say sorry to God for their sins that can mess up this world.

TOWER OF BABEL

Materials Needed
✔ set of blocks
✔ television or radio
✔ stuffed animals

Setting the Stage
The lesson you want to communicate to your children is that there is only one way to get to God and that is through Jesus' death on the cross. In this story the people tried to get to God another way and it didn't work.

Project
1. Take a set of blocks and lay them out on the floor. The object of the game is to try to build a tower, **but the children are not to know this yet**. Explain to them that for the next few minutes they are only allowed to talk "gibberish," which is a made up language that no one else can understand. Say "Go" and have everyone talk gibberish at the same time while trying to do something with the blocks. When you say "Stop," see what has been built. If they seem to be making good progress during the "gibberish" time, you might need to misdirect them a bit. The point to make is that when you can't understand each other it is very difficult to build something. **Now** let them know that they were to be building a tower.

2. Move to a television or radio and turn it on to a station where a different language is being spoken, a language no one in the house can understand. It would be best if you had already located the station ahead of time so the children will not be distracted with the other programs. Point out to them how hard it is to understand what is being said in this other language.

3. It would be fun for the older children to learn the word "thank you" in several different languages. Here are some examples:
    Spanish - Gracias
    German - Danke
    French - Merci
    Italian - Grazie

4. Tell the story of the tower of Babel as found in Genesis 11. The people spoke one language and they decided they were going to build a tower to get to God their own way. God was not happy with this, so he caused them all to speak a different language. When they could not understand each other they had to stop building. Remind the children how they felt earlier when they could not understand each other while building. People who could understand each other grouped together and moved off to an area of their own. The lesson they needed to learn was that there is only one way to get to God and that is through Jesus Christ.

Memory Verse

John 14:6

Jesus answered, "I am the way and the truth and the life. No one comes to the Father except through me."

Sit in a circle with an adult holding the stuffed animal. Explain that when you are holding the stuffed animal it is your turn to say the verse. When you toss it to somebody else it is their turn to say the verse. Continue the game, speeding up as you go along, until everyone can say the verse easily. Note: The three year old might have difficulty mastering the verse so the game will need to be slowed down for him or her.

Prayer

Thank God for sending Jesus to die on the cross for our sins. Let God know you understand that the only way to Heaven is by saying thank you for Jesus' death. Note: The older children can also pray and say they are sorry for their sins. You may explain to the older children that it is not just saying the words "Thank you" but you also have to believe in your heart that you can't get into Heaven by just being good; it is only through Jesus' gift of eternal life.

LOT'S ESCAPE

Materials Needed
✔ Different colors of modeling clay or playdough

Setting the Stage
There are times when each member of the family is tempted to do something wrong. During those times we need to learn to say " No" and if necessary even run away from the temptation. In Genesis 19 we see Lot running and his wife looking back longingly.

Project
The first part of the project involves making people out of clay or playdough. These are the characters and items that need to be made. Use your imagination to make them come alive.

Lot	angel
Lot's two daughters	house
Lot's wife	hill

Now it is time for the adult to tell the story using your clay people.

Scene I (House, Lot and Angel)

Lot: (beside the house) This city is so bad. No one obeys God.

Angel: Yes, Lot, that is the reason why God is going to destroy the whole city with fire.

Lot: What about me and my family?

Angel: You are the only ones who love God, and so I am here to tell you to run out of the city as fast as you can and go up into the hills. The one rule is "Don't look back as you run or you will turn into a pillar of salt."

Scene II (Lot, Lot's wife, Lot's two daughters)

Lot: We need to leave this city right away because God is going to destroy it with fire.

D.#1:   Okay, dad, we will obey God and go.

D.#2:   Do I have to pack all my toys?

Lot: No, just pack your pajamas and a change of clothes because we can't waste any time.

Wife: Wait a minute, Lot, do you think that God really means what he said? I really love this house, and all my friends are here, and I really don't want to go.

Lot: Yes, he meant what he said and he even told us "Don't look back" because looking back will show you really want to stay rather than obey God.

Wife: Okay, I hear you.

Scene III (Lot, Lot's Wife, Lot's two daughters and hill)

(everybody is running up the hill)

Lot: Come on and don't look back!

Wife: I can't obey God because I really want to look back (she turns and looks back and freezes like a pillar of salt)

D.#1:   Dad, Mom is a pillar of salt!

D.#2:   Dad, shouldn't we stop for Mom?

Lot: I am sorry about your mother, but you both need to obey God and keep running. No, we will have to leave her there.

Story ends with Lot and his two daughters on top of the hill. The city does burn and Lot understands that it was good they ran away and obeyed God.

Song

"Lot Must Run"
(use the tune to "Three Blind Mice")
Lot must run, Lot must run. Run away from sin. Up the mountain he was to go, not to look back down below, he had to learn to say, "No!" Lot must run.

Prayer

Pray about something you are tempted to do but you know you shouldn't. Ask God to help you say, "No!" to that temptation. Also ask God for the willingness to run away just as Lot did if that is the only way to obey God and not do something wrong.

JOSEPH

Materials Needed
✔ large bowl of chocolate or caramel instant pudding (milk)
✔ one large zip-lock bag or a large clear plastic bag with a twist tie
✔ 8 1/2" x 11" piece of white paper
✔ a small bowl and spoon for each person

Setting the Stage
In *Genesis 37 and 39 - 45*, we see how Joseph learned the three principles of patience, trusting God and forgiveness. As you tell this story you will want to emphasize when Joseph learned these principles and that we need to do the same.

Project
Ahead of time make the pudding following the directions on the box. Fill the plastic bag with three table-spoons of pudding and tightly secure the opening. Put the rest of the pudding in small bowls for each person to eat while the story is being told. Place the bag on the sheet of paper and smooth the pudding. The pudding should cover the entire surface. When you run your finger across the top of the bag, a white line should remain there. If this does not happen add or take away some of the pudding until you have the desired effect. Draw with your finger the designated picture on top of the bag as you tell the corresponding part of the story.

 ✎ Joseph had eleven brothers. His dad liked him so much he gave Joseph a coat of many colors to show everyone that Joseph was his favorite son. This made the brothers very angry. To top it off, Joseph told his brothers twice that he had a dream where the brother bowed down to him as if he were a king or something. The brothers were so upset they decided to sell Joseph. Joseph became a slave in a far away land called Egypt.

 ✎ Joseph worked hard and his owner liked him very much until one day the owner's wife said that Joseph had done something he really didn't do. Even though the wife was lying Joseph's owner had Joseph thrown into jail.

 ✎ While Joseph was in jail two men who worked for the Pharaoh (the Pharaoh was another name for a king) were also thrown into jail. While they were there they had dreams, and with God's help Joseph told them what their dreams meant. When one of the men returned to the Pharaoh to continue to work for him, Joseph asked the man to remember him because Joseph was hoping to get out of jail. A long time passed and Joseph never heard anything or got any help getting out of jail. This would have been very hard on Joseph. During this time Joseph not only learned patience but also how to trust God. Joseph knew God had a plan for his life and that God had not forgotten him in jail.

 ✎ Eventually Pharaoh started to have some dreams that really upset him. Pharaoh wanted to know what they meant. They were dreams about cows and baskets of bread with birds eating the bread. No one could tell the Pharaoh what the dreams meant until the man who had been freed from jail remembered Joseph.

Joseph told the Pharaoh what the dreams meant. Joseph even told the Pharaoh what to do so that in years to come they would still have a lot of food. The Pharaoh was so happy he made Joseph his right-hand man. Joseph was now like a prince.

Meanwhile in another land Joseph's brothers had run out of food. They decided to go to Egypt and see if they could get some food. When they got there they were brought to Joseph. Joseph recognized his brothers right away, but the brothers didn't recognize Joseph because they expected him to be a slave, not a prince. The brothers bowed down before Joseph (just as they did in the dream Joseph had a long time ago). Then the brothers asked for some food. Now the brothers had been very mean to Joseph, but Joseph decided to forgive them. That would have been a very hard thing to do, but it was the best thing to do. Joseph did forgive and they became a family again. They all lived in Egypt together.

Song

"Trust and Obey"
(use original tune or create own tune).
Trust and obey for there is no other way to be happy in Jesus but to trust and obey.

Prayer

Ask God to help you be like Joseph so you too can learn to be patient, to trust God and to forgive.

BABY MOSES

Materials Needed

- ✔ brown construction paper (1 sheet per person)
- ✔ glue
- ✔ small bowl or round-bottomed cup
- ✔ white paper
- ✔ scissors
- ✔ small scraps of material
- ✔ crayons
- ✔ children's Bible

Setting the Stage

God looks out for us just as he did for baby Moses. As you are putting together the basket as well as making baby Moses, take the time to show each child that he or she is loved and cared for by God.

Project

The end product will be a brown basket lined with a scrap of material and a paper doll that serves as Baby Moses. While you are working on the project you can read the story from a children's Bible or tell it in your own words. The story is found in *Exodus 2: 1-10*.

Details to include when telling the story.

- ◗ There were so many of Joseph's descendants, (called Hebrews) in the land of Egypt that the Egyptians decided to make them all slaves. Even so the Hebrews were still so many that the Pharaoh (not the Pharaoh from Joseph's day) ordered all the baby boys to be killed.
- ◗ Moses was born during this time and God was looking after Moses. Moses' mother put him in a basket and hid him in the reeds beside a river. It was not long before the Pharaoh's daughter came down to the river to take a bath. When she heard the baby crying she fell in love with the little boy and wanted the baby to be her own son.
- ◗ Moses still got to go back to his own mother for a few years. During this time Moses' mother taught him about God. Then it was time for Moses to go and live in the palace with the Pharaoh's daughter.

The way to make the basket and baby.

- ◗ Cut the brown construction paper into 1 inch strips
- ◗ Weave the strips together making sure that you put a drop of glue wherever two strips touch each other.
- ◗ Follow the diagram to make the weaving easier.
- ◗ Continue the weaving until you have a large enough space to curve and form a small basket.
- ◗ While the glue is still wet curve the woven paper over the bottom of the cup or bowl.
- ◗ Cut out a small paper doll and color it to look like a baby.
- ◗ Once the glue is dry, trim the excess brown paper to give the bowl the appearance of a basket.
- ◗ Line the basket with a scrap of material and place the doll inside.

Memory Verse

Jeremiah 29:11
" For I know the plans I have for you," declares the LORD.

While reviewing the verse talk about the plans God has for each one of you and how he will look after us just as he looked after Moses.

Prayer

Thank God for looking after each one of you.

MOSES THE LEADER

Materials Needed
- ✔ one hanger per child
- ✔ construction paper in red, green, brown, black and white
- ✔ a hole punch or sharp object
- ✔ string

Setting the Stage
Moses did become the leader who freed the Jews from their slavery in Egypt. During this lesson you need to communicate to your children that Moses was a good leader for God even during the difficult times. The telling of this story is found in Exodus 5 - 12.

Project
Your children will be making a mobile with the ten plagues hanging from the hanger. Each plague will have a picture the child has drawn, colored and cut out. A hole is punched in the top of the cutout and a string threaded through and knotted. Tie the other end of the string to the bottom of the hanger. Each cutout should be hanging at a different level.

Explain:
- ✍ Moses went before the Pharaoh and said, (adult calls out) "Let my people go!!" Pharaoh said, (together have the children call out) "NO!!"
- ✍ Because Pharaoh would not obey God, God had to send some plagues. Those who loved God were not affected by the plagues. But those who did not want to obey God suffered because of the plagues.

Below are the plagues, drawings to be made and dialogue that needs to occur. Note: While cutting out each plague, discuss with your children why each event would be so terrible.

Plague 1. The river which was their water source was turned to blood
(cut out a one inch curvy strip of red paper)

Adult - "Moses again said, 'Let my people go!' but the Pharaoh said..."   **Children** - "No!"

Plague 2. Frogs all over
(a green frog)

Adult - "Moses again said, 'Let my people go!' but the Pharaoh said..."   **Children** - "No!"

Plague 3. So many gnats that it was hard for people to breathe
(small, brown flying creature)

Adult - "Moses again said, 'Let my people go!' but the Pharaoh said..."   **Children** - "No!"

Plague 4. Swarms of flies
(black paper)

Adult - "Moses again said, 'Let my people go!' but the Pharaoh said..."   **Children** - "No!"

Plague 5. Cows all got sick and died
(white paper on which black spots are drawn)

> **Adult** - "Moses again said, 'Let my people go!' but the Pharaoh said..."
> **Children** - "No!"

Plague 6. Oozing sores all over the body
(white paper doll figure with colored sores)

> **Adult** - "Moses again said, 'Let my people go!' but the Pharaoh said..."
> **Children** - "No!"

Plague 7. Hail and fire that destroyed their food and their homes
(red for the fire and white for the hail)

> **Adult** - "Moses again said, 'Let my people go!' but the Pharaoh said..."
> **Children** - "No!"

Plague 8. Locust which ate the rest of their crop
(green in color but it looks like a beetle with larger wings)

> **Adult** - "Moses again said, 'Let my people go!' but the Pharaoh said..."
> **Children** - "No!"

Plague 9. Darkness that was so dark you couldn't see or do anything.
(black cloud)

> **Adult** - "Moses again said, 'Let my people go!' but the Pharaoh said..."
> **Children** - "No!"

Plague 10. Death of the first born son
(white paper doll with his eyes closed)

Note: These plagues did not happen to anyone who was willing to obey what God asked, but Pharaoh did not obey. Pharaoh's first-born son did die and finally the Pharaoh let the Hebrews go. If the Pharaoh had obeyed God none of this would have happened. Moses did obey God even though many people were very angry with him. In the end it was wonderful because the Hebrews were free to go to their own land. It was good that Moses was a leader for God.

Prayer
Ask God to help each of you be a leader for God with each of your own friends.

JERICHO

Materials Needed

✔ different colored sheets of construction paper
✔ magazines with lots of pictures (one per child)
✔ stapler or tape
✔ markers or colored pencils
✔ scissors
✔ glue

Setting the Stage

As a family you are constructing a magazine that could have been made by the people inside the wall of Jericho. In Joshua chapters 2, 3 and 6 we see the Israelites finally coming to take over their land - the land that God had given them. The people in this land were not willing to follow God. Except for Rahab. You will want the pages to illustrate how the people felt as they waited to see what was going to happen. The lesson is for everyone and will remind your children how important it is to be on God's side.

Project

Each person receives a piece of construction paper and a magazine. A pair of scissors and some glue will need to be shared among you. Each person is to receive an assignment chosen from the ideas section below. Look through the magazines to find a picture that best depicts the emotion of the person for whom your child is writing. Only the picture is necessary, but if the older children would like to write a sentence or two, you will find some ideas below.

Details:

Before you begin the magazine you need to share a few details about the story with your children.

✗ God was giving the land to the Israelites. The people there needed to side with God and obey God, but they didn't want to do that.

✗ The first city the Israelites were to take over was Jericho. Jericho had a huge wall around it and when the gate was closed no one could get in or out.

✗ Spies were sent to see what the city was like. Rahab, a woman inside the city of Jericho, decided to side with God so she hid the spies. She helped them escape in a basket down the side of the wall.

✗ Rahab was told she would be saved along with her family.

✗ Rahab had to wait for a while and keep a red piece of cloth hanging out of her window so the Israelites would know which place was hers.

✗ The Israelites set up camp outside the walls and started to march around the walls every day.

✗ The Israelites were told by God to sound the trumpets and the walls would fall down. The city of Jericho would be theirs.

Ideas:

1. "How Strong Are Our Walls?" written by the Gate Watchman
(Picture of a worried man, lego blocks, wooden blocks, fence around a yard)

> Older children can write a few sentences about how the watchman might feel anxious about whether the bricks are strong enough or if there is a hole in the wall.

2. "How Did They Get Away?" written by the Policeman
(Picture of a policeman, boys or men running, someone peeking around a corner, a room with no one in it)

> Older children can explain how the policeman is concerned that he let the spies get back home without catching them.

3. "The Trumpets Will Sound" written by the Court Composer.
(Picture of any musical instruments, someone singing, people marching in a row)

> Older children can talk about how loud it will be when the trumpets blow and what will happen when the walls fall down.

4. "Waiting, How Hard It Is!" written by Rahab.
(Picture of a basket, rope, red piece of material, woman looking for something, someone sitting and waiting)

> Older children will understand that Rahab sided with God, but now she has to wait inside the walls until God sends the men for her. She has to be patient and trust God. Let them write about that.

5. Make up your own. There are also the points of view of Rahab's family, the king, the army who wants to fight or the common person who does not understand what is happening.

Finished Product:
Make a cover for your magazine. The magazine could be called "The Jericho Wall". Put it together with a stapler or tape. When it is all together, take the time to read it as a family and talk about the fact that the Jews outside the camp were concerned as well, but they had sided with God and they knew that they could trust God.

Finish the devotional by sharing with the children these details:
- The wall did fall down when the trumpets blew.
- God did give the city to the Israelites without them even having to raise a sword.
- Rahab did go to live with the Israelites.
- Years later we see that Rahab became the great, great grandmother of King David.

Prayer
"Help me learn to side with you, because I know that in the end you always win!"

GIDEON

Materials Needed

- ✔ pebbles or tiny wads of paper (15 per child)
- ✔ glue
- ✔ 2" x 2" piece of cardboard (one per child)

Setting the Stage

There comes a point in everyone's life when they find it easy to relate to Gideon. Gideon was a man who was faced with a frightening situation. His immediate reaction was cowardly, but whenhe saw God's power and accepted God's strength he bravely faced the challenge. During this devotional you will help your children understand that there are frightening situations we try to face alone.When we know that God is with us, we can bravely face these same circumstances.

Project

#1 Mimes

Each person is to think of a situation that frightens them. If a younger child needs help, whisper some ideas in his/her ear and let the child choose. Once each person has decided on a situation, take turns pan-tomiming each choice. The rest of the family will try to guess what each situation is. When everyone has had a turn, discuss each situation so the children will remember their choice throughout the remainder of the devotional.

Note: An adult should go first to demonstrate to the children what they need to do. Younger children might need to use some words to communicate their chosen situation.

#2 Places to cook

Ask the children to find all the places where you can cook a meal in the house. Have them take you for a tour to point out each place.

      Examples: stove   barbecue   fireplace

                 microwave   camp stove

Have them list any other cooking locations not found in your home. When they have finished the list ask them if someone could cook meat on a big stone. Pretend you are convinced of this possibility. When they become adamant that this couldn't happen, have them sit down and share the following story about a time when a stone was a place for cooking.

#3 Story of Gideon from Judges 6

This is a story about a man who was very afraid in a situation just like we are sometimes. Gideon and his people were being cruelly ruled by the Midianites. The Midianites were a group of people who were bullies; they were always stealing and hurting the Hebrews. An angel of the Lord came to tell Gideon to stop these bad people. The angel found Gideon hiding from the Midianites instead of being brave.   Gideon was so afraid he told God, "I am the smallest and the weakest and I can't do it!" He needed to see God do something to show his power. The angel told Gideon to put the meat and sauce he had on a rock. The angel touched the rock with his staff and fire came out of the rock, burning the meat. When Gideon saw this he knew that God could do anything. Gideon went out, destroyed his enemy's altar and built an altar to God to show that God was with him. The bullies were amazed at how brave Gideon was and eventually they stopped being mean.

#4 Discuss

Ask your children the following questions:
> ➤ Like Gideon you are afraid in a certain situation.
>> What situation did you act out earlier that makes you afraid?
> ➤ God showed his strength to Gideon by burning the food on the stone.
>> How does God show his strength to you?
> ➤ What did Gideon build to show the bad people that God was with him?

#5 Build an Altar

Each of you will build a little altar as a reminder this week that God is with you. As you face the situation that makes you afraid, remember to be brave in God.
> a) Glue seven pebbles in a small circle on the center of your piece of cardboard.
> b) Glue five pebbles on top of the seven allowing the circle to be a little smaller.
> c) Glue three pebbles on top of the five again allowing the circle to be smaller.

Make sure the glue dries before you move it.

Prayer

Have each child pray for their own...
> ... fearful situation
> ... way in which they have seen God work
> ... approach to the situation with God's help.

Memory Verse

Judges 6:16a
The Lord answered, "I will be with you."

RUTH

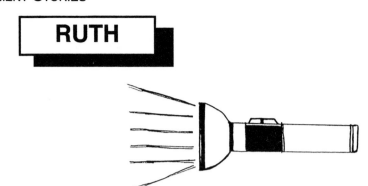

Materials Needed
- ✔ flashlight
- ✔ piece of white paper
- ✔ crayons
- ✔ dress-up clothes (optional)

Setting the Stage
You will literally be doing just that — setting the stage — for an old fashioned movie. The effect is quite good and easily achieved. All the lights are turned off. An adult holds the flashlight and shakes it very quickly back and forth on the person acting. To make it look like an old fashioned movie the person acting must say their lines while jumping or wiggling. The purpose of all this fun is to communicate that we need to make God our God just as Ruth did in the book of Ruth.

Project
There are three or possibly four roles in this movie. Children may put on dress-up clothes to add color to their role playing. If there is a shortage of people, make this devotional a "family and friends devotional" so their friends can be a part of the experience.

Note: An adult will need to tell the children their lines and allow them time to repeat each line while acting.

Ruth   a foreigner whose husband has died. She is returning with her mother-in-law to Naomi's homeland.

Naomi   Ruth's mother-in-law whose husband and sons have died and is returning to her homeland.

Boaz   a relative of Naomi's who is very rich and eventually falls in love with Ruth.

Extra   person in the city who is mean to Ruth and is also a worker in the fields for Boaz.

Lights off and a darkened room. Flashlight on. Stage ready for the first act. (Note: Hold the flashlight still between acts. When the players are in position start wiggling it again.)

Act I (Naomi and Ruth)
Naomi: I have to go home. I no longer have a husband or sons, boo hoo!!
Ruth: I will go with you.
Naomi: But you don't know anyone there.
Ruth: I will make your people my people and your God my God
Naomi: Okay, let's go!

Act II (Ruth, Naomi, and Extra)
Naomi: We're home!
Extra: OOOO! Who is that girl with Naomi? We don't want her here!
Ruth: The people are not very nice to me, but I still want to make your people my people and your God my God.
Naomi: Well, I am too old to work, so you will have to go work in the fields.
Ruth: Okay, here I go!

Act III (Ruth, Boaz and Extra)

Ruth: It has been a long day picking up this food, but I know Naomi will be happy with all I have.

Boaz: That girl Ruth is a hard worker. I will have to tell my men to make sure to leave her lots of food.

Extra: Here, Ruth, have some more food. Boaz, my boss, thinks you are a hard worker.

Act IV (Ruth and Naomi)

Ruth: Look, Naomi, I have lots of food. Boaz was looking after me.

Naomi: Boaz? Why he is a relative of mine. You know you should marry him. He would make a good husband.

Ruth: I would love to marry Boaz.

Act V

Ruth: You are very kind, Boaz

Boaz: You need a husband, and I would like to be your husband but there are some people I will have to talk to first.

Ruth: That is fine.

Boaz: I will talk to the people, and then I will let you know.

Act VI (Ruth, Boaz, and Naomi)

Boaz: Yes, everything worked out and I can marry you.

Ruth: Wonderful! I knew God would look after me.

Naomi: That is because you made my God your God.

The End (everyone takes a bow)

Memory Verse

Ruth 1:16b

Your people will be my people and your God my God.

On a piece of paper write this verse in the following way using a crayon and some creative drawings.

Your (picture of a person) will be my (picture of a person) and

Your (drawing of a crown) my (drawing of a crown).

Hang this on the fridge so you can review this verse throughout the week.

Prayer

We need to be like Ruth and make God our God. There are lots of things we can put before God (friends, television, toys), but if we want God to be first in our lives we need to make Him the most important person. Now is a good time to talk to God about this.

KING DAVID

Materials Needed

✔ five paper plates or five pieces of construction paper
✔ string
✔ hole punch or pointed object
✔ markers or crayons
✔ scissors

Setting the Stage

Nothing is impossible with God. In this story found in I Samuel 17, we see that David was able to kill a lion and a giant because God helped him. The story will be acted out by the members of the family, but first you will take some time to make five different masks.

Project

The masks can be drawn on the paper plates or you can cut the pieces of construction paper the size of the paper plate and use that. Once the face is drawn, holes need to be punched on either side near the middle so the string can fit around the head just above the ear. Make sure not to punch the holes too close to the edge or the plate will rip. You will need to take some time to adjust the string to the child's head before you knot it in the second hole. These are the five masks to be made.

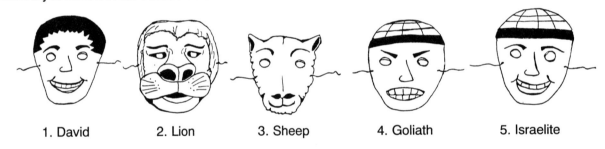

| 1. David | 2. Lion | 3. Sheep | 4. Goliath | 5. Israelite |

There are three scenes to be acted. Whoever is playing a particular role needs to wear the appropriate mask for those lines. Some roles can be doubled (played by one person). For example, one person can play the lion and the Israelite and another person can play the sheep and Goliath.
Note: An adult will need to tell the children their lines and allow the children time to repeat the lines while acting.

Scene 1: David looking after the sheep (David, Sheep, Lion)

Sheep:	Baa, Baa.
David:	(singing to God) "Jesus loves me this I know..."
Lion:	Roar - I am going to eat a sheep.
Sheep:	Help! Help!
David:	Help me, God! (takes out his pretend sling shot and swings it over his head. He lets go and everyone watches the pretend rock fly through the air and hit the lion.)
Lion:	Ouch! (dies lying on the ground)
David:	Thank you, God, for helping me save the sheep from the lion.

Scene 2: David fighting Goliath the giant, an enemy of the Israelites
(David, Goliath, Israelite)

Goliath: (yells) Who will come and fight me?
David: Why won't anybody fight Goliath? God would help that person, I know!
Israelite: He is so big and we are so little and everyone is afraid.
David: Well, I am not afraid and I know God will help me.
Goliath: (yells) Who will come and fight me?
David: I will!
Goliath: What? You're only a boy!
David: Yes, but God will help me (David takes out his pretend sling shot and swings it over his head. He lets go and everyone watches the pretend rock fly through the air and hit Goliath on the head)
Goliath: Good shot - I guess God did help you! (grabs his head and falls down dead)
Israelite: Yea David, Yea God!!

Scene 3: David Made King (David, Israelite)

David: (kneels down on his knees) Yes, I will be king with God's help.
Israelite: (taps David's head) You are crowned king.
David: I am glad that God has helped me because nothing is impossible for God.

The End

Song

"Only a Boy Named David"
(use original tune or do it in a chant style with a catchy beat)

Only a boy named David, only a little sling, only a boy named David, but he could pray and sing. Only a boy named David, only a rippling brook. Only a boy named David, but five little stones he took. And one little stone went in the sling and the sling went round and round. One little stone went in the sling and the sling went round and round. Round and round and round and round and round and round and round. One little stone went through the air and the giant came tumbling down.

Memory Verse

Luke 1:37
For nothing is impossible with God.

Prayer

In his or her own words let each person communicate this thought to God: "When I have a tough job to do I should not try to do it in my own strength but with your help, God."

ELIJAH

Materials Needed

✔ four or more large house plants or kitchen chairs
✔ large couch cushions or blankets
   a bowl of your favorite finger food as a snack (example: a bunch of green grapes)

Setting the Stage

God provides help in strange ways. You can see this truth very clearly in the story of Elijah. Turn your living room into a ravine oasis. The plants can line a pretend stream or the chairs and cushions can act like ravine walls with the pretend stream running down the middle.

Project

Pretend you are Elijah. Before you enter the ravine oasis explain to the children that Elijah was a man who loved God and God gave him messages to tell other people. Sometimes his messages made these people angry. In our story some people were so angry at Elijah they tried to kill him.

The details of this story are in I Kings 17.

Elijah was running and running

> Everyone runs in place.

Finally he came to a ravine with an oasis where he could hide.

> Get down on your knees and crawl into the ravine making sure you don't get wet from the water in the pretend stream.

Elijah was so glad to be there. I bet the first thing he did was to take a drink of the water.

> All lean over and scoop up some pretend water in the palm of your hand and sip it.

Elijah would be so thankful to God that I am sure he would want to sing to God.

> At this time sing your favorite song to God; one you all know from Sunday school or one that you have learned in these devotionals.

After Elijah sang do you think he told God, "Thank you"? I am sure he did and so pretending we are Elijah let's say thank you.

> Let each person say a few words in thanks. Example: Thanks for the water. Thanks for keeping me safe, etc.

After a little while Elijah probably started to get hungry, but look around. There doesn't seem to be anything to eat. Who do you think brought the food to Elijah?

> Start making bird sounds until they say the right answer.

That's right, it was the birds. God knew Elijah needed to eat and there was no food here, so God sent the food.

> As they are guessing birds, pretend you are a bird and fly to where you have hidden the bowl of finger food. Fly back to the group with the food and let them enjoy it.

Elijah was safe, and even after he finally left this special place, God continued to keep Elijah safe.

Song
Sing your favorite praise song to God. You can repeat the one you sang earlier or you can sing another favorite.

Prayer
Thank God for the way he takes care of each one of you. If you have specific examples now would be a good time to share them. Thank God specifically for them.

ESTHER

Materials Needed
✔ food for a meal or a snack
✔ table and chairs for a pretend restaurant

Setting the Stage
In the book of Esther we hear of an incredible thing that happened in the land. A young Jewish girl has just become the queen. This young girl's name is Esther, and she does some wonderful things. During the serving of food the adult, who is the server, will share the details of the story. The lesson here is that no matter how young you are you can be used by God to do some very special things for other people.

Project
This can be tea time or meal time. Some ideas for what to serve are suggested below, but you may use your own favorites. Make sure that whatever you serve you do it in stages so you can tell the story in stages

First course: Small bowl of favorite soup
Server's story (told as you serve. Speak enthusiastically as if you have a great secret you want to share): "Have you heard about that young teenager, Esther? The one who is now queen? Did you know that she is probably only 13 or 14 years old? Well, the king sure thinks she is beautiful. Did you know she won the position of queen by winning a sort of beauty contest? There were lots of girls who wanted to win, but Esther was so beautiful and nice the king loved her the first time he saw her. Well, enjoy your meal!"

Second course: Fruit pieces or salad
Server's story: "Was your soup good? While I serve you the next part let me tell you what happened. No one knew that Esther was a Jew. You see Esther's uncle, Mordecai, told her not to tell anyone that she was a Jew. Of course, Mordecai was a Jew as well. Mordecai hung around the castle in case Esther needed him. It was during this time the king's right-hand man, Haman, got angry at Mordecai. Haman decided not only to kill Mordecai but to kill all the Jews. He asked the king if it was okay, and the king passed a law that on one day all the Jews were to be killed. Now this was a problem because, of course, the queen was a Jew too!! I'll tell you more when I am back with the next part of your meal."

Third course: Hot dogs with potato chips
Server's story: "Are you wondering what Queen Esther is going to do? Well, I think she wondered too, but she got a message from her Uncle Mordecai and he reminded her that God had given her the position of Queen so she could help other people. The problem was if Esther went to the king and told him that she too was a Jew, she could die. If she didn't say anything, then all the Jews would die, but she might not die because no one knew she was a Jew. That would be a hard decision to make, wouldn't it?

Fourth course: Ice Cream
Server's story: "I don't want to make you wait any longer to find out what happened. The queen went to the king and the king was glad she told him about the situation. The king was so upset with Haman that he had Haman killed. The king changed the law so the Jews didn't have to die after all. That was a tough job for Queen Esther to do, but I am sure glad she did it because I have a lot of friends who are Jews. Well, enjoy the rest of the meal and I will be back to get your money when you are done."

Pay Time $$$
As you collect the pretend money, challenge each person to learn to be like Queen Esther. Ask each one how they can help a person in their life. Remember each response.

Prayer
When you are finished collecting the money, stop and say a prayer for each person around the table. In the prayer ask God to help them help the child mentioned earlier so they will be like Queen Esther.

DANIEL AND THE LION'S DEN

Materials Needed

- ✔ toothpicks
- ✔ four small bowls and a spoon
- ✔ food coloring

Recipe for Icing
- ✍ 1 1/2 tablespoons margarine
- ✍ 1 1/2 tablespoons milk
- ✍ 1/2 teaspoon vanilla
- ✍ 1 cup icing sugar

Blend the above ingredients together while slowly adding the icing sugar. Separate the icing into four equal portions. Place each portion into separate small bowls and add a different color of food coloring to each bowl. Stir until the color is uniform.

Recipe for Sugar Cookies
- ✍ 1/2 cup margarine
- ✍ 1 cup sugar
- ✍ 2 eggs
- ✍ 2 tablespoons milk
- ✍ 2 1/2 cups flour
- ✍ 1 1/2 teaspoons baking powder
- ✍ 1/4 teaspoon salt
- ✍ 1 teaspoon vanilla

Cream together the margarine and sugar. Add the eggs. Beat until smooth. Add the milk and vanilla. Mix together the flour, baking powder and salt. Add the dry ingredients to the wet ingredients and blend until smooth. Lightly flour your counter top and roll your dough until it is 1/4 inch thick. Cut the cookies into the shape of Daniel, King, two or more bad men and two or more lions using a dull knife and your imagination. Bake them at 375º F for 10 minutes. Remove from the oven and cool before using.

Setting the Stage
Sometimes we can go through a whole day and not even think about taking time to pray to our God. In this story found in Daniel 6 we see that Daniel has the privilege of praying taken away from him. Daniel's response is a commitment to pray, no matter what. This should be our motto and one you will want to communicate to your family.

Project
Once the cookies have cooled you can begin devotions. Have the cookies, bowls of icing and toothpicks on the table. Let each person choose a person or an animal cookie shape. Not only will they decorate the shape they have chosen, but they will also play that same role as the story is being enacted.
You can give them the details of the story while you are decorating the cookies.

Details:
Daniel was a Jew who was a captive in one country while his family lived in another country. He
✗ was such a smart man he was asked to help the king a lot. Even though Daniel was a long way from home, he had not forgotten God.

Daniel loved to talk to God and everyone knew it. If you looked inside his window you could see
✗ him kneeling down to pray. He did this three times a day.

✗ A bunch of men who also worked for the king did not like Daniel and they wanted to kill him. So they tricked the king into making a rule that no one was allowed to pray to anyone except the king. If anyone disobeyed this rule they were to be thrown into the lions' den to be eaten by the lions.

✗ Daniel could not obey the rule because he loved to pray to God. So Daniel was thrown into the den of lions. This made the king sad since he really did like Daniel, but a rule is a rule and even the king could not break his own rule.

✗ Surprise!! The lions did not eat Daniel because God closed their mouths. The next morning the king found out Daniel was alive and he was so happy. The king decided to throw the bad men into the lion's den and those men were all eaten by the lions.

✗ The king then made a new rule that everyone was to pray to Daniel's God because he was the real God.

Drama:

- By now the cookies should be decorated and you all should be ready to act out the story.
- Keep the acting simple. You can give them the idea and let them try to figure out what to say.
- Have Daniel praying and the bad men talking about wanting to kill Daniel.
- The bad men are with the king making the rule about only praying to the king.
- Daniel says he will still pray to God.
- Daniel is thrown into the lion's den and the king is sad.
- The next day Daniel is still alive and the king is happy.
- The king throws the bad men into the lions' den and they are eaten.
- The king makes the new rule that everyone is to pray to Daniel's God.

Once the story is over, enjoy eating the cookies together.

Song

"One Little, Two Little, Three Little Lions"
(use the tune of "One Little Two Little Three Little Indians")
One little, two little, three little lions, four little, five little, six little lions, seven little, eight little, nine little lions, ten little lions in a den

The adult calls out, "Did they eat Daniel?" In response the children call, "No!".

Prayer
Ask God to help you remember to pray to Him everyday this week.

JONAH

Materials Needed

✔ partially-filled bathtub or sink
✔ large sponge or plastic bowl
✔ three small plastic or paper people
✔ pretend money
✔ grapes

Setting the Stage

The lesson you want to communicate is that when people are bad we need to help them to be good instead of being happy when they get punished. Talk about this lesson before starting on the project.

Project

1. The adult will play the role of coordinator and everyone else will pretend to be Jonah. Have each room set up beforehand so you can move from station to station without interruptions. Make sure each child has some pretend money in a pocket.

> Explain to them that they are about to experience what Jonah did in the story as recorded in the Bible in the book of Jonah. When it comes time for the children to say their lines, tell them what to say and have them repeat it.

2. **Kitchen (Jonah's Home)** - Adult plays God and stands on kitchen chair. Others pretend to be Jonah, who is fixing dinner.
   Adult calls out: "Jonah, go to Nineveh and tell the people that I am sad they are bad."
   Children call out: "No, those people are mean."
   Adult says: "Jonah decided to go to Joppa and from there take a boat to another city called Tarshish, which was a long way from Nineveh."

> Together run to the bathroom where the boat awaits you.

   Children call out while running: "I'm not going to obey God."

3. **Bathroom (Port at Joppa)** - Have everyone stand around the tub or sink. Large sponge or plastic bowl is the boat. Adult, have each child pay you pretend money.
   Children say: "Ticket for Tarshish please."

> Once everyone has a ticket, explain that the three plastic or paper people are Jonah and two boatmen. For the rest of this section have the plastic people act out the scene with the adult saying the lines.

   Jonah: "Excuse me, here is my ticket. May I please go on the boat?"
   Boatmen: "Sure, hop on."
   Jonah: "Disobeying God has made me tired, so I think I will lie down and go to sleep. God will never find me here."

> Put all three onto the sponge or bowl and push them into the middle of the water. Explain that they set sail and soon a big storm came. Have the children lightly splash waster onto the boat so that it causes a storm in the tub.

Boatmen: "Why is God sending such a storm? Someone must have done something wrong. Let's draw straws, and whoever gets the short straw must be the one that has upset God."

> Explain that they all drew straws and Jonah got the short one.

Jonah: "Sorry men, I have disobeyed God. Just throw me over the edge of the boat into the water and the storm will stop. "

> Explain that this is what they did, then drop the plastic Jonah into the water. Switch roles. The children are to pretend that they are in the water. Have the children hold their breath and swim to the bedroom.

4. **Bedroom (inside big fish)** - Climb onto the bed. Leave the light off and door slightly open so there is only a little light entering the room.

> Explain that everybody has just been swallowed by a big fish and you are in the fish's stomach, so you can now breathe (let breath out). Have everyone comment on what it would be like to be in the stomach of a big fish (dark, wet, smelly).

Adult says: "Now, once Jonah realized that he was inside a fish, he knew God had sent this fish to save him. But Jonah still had to stay inside the fish for three days. What do you think Jonah did for those three days?"

> Allow the children to give their answers, but try to encourage at least one of them to say 'talked to God' or 'prayed' because that is exactly what he did. Have everyone get on their knees, on top of the bed, and have each child say a sentence prayer, one that they think Jonah might have said (guide them when necessary). Then have everyone go to the door and explain that God made the fish sick and the fish spit Jonah out onto the beach. Say 1, 2, 3 open the door and let everybody jump out of the bedroom and onto the "beach" ready to walk to Nineveh.

5. **Living Room (Nineveh)** - Walk around the living room, as Jonah would have walked around Nineveh, calling out the message over and over to the people.
Children call out: "Say you're sorry to God. You shouldn't be so mean."

> Everyone walks over to the couch and climbs up on it.

Adult says: "Jonah really didn't think the people were going to say they were sorry. He was sure God would punish them instead. So he was just going to sit up on a hill and watch what God was going to do to them. You know, while he watched, God let a vine grow over him to give him shade. Let's pretend it was a grape vine and enjoy some of the grapes."

> Bring out the bowl of grapes and eat them while discussing what God is probably going to do.

Adult says: "You know what? The people said they were sorry so God forgave them. That made Jonah angry. God told Jonah he should be happy because the people didn't get punished. Eventually Jonah realized that was true."

> Review the lesson mentioned in "Setting the Stage." Ask each child to think of one person he/she can help this week.

Prayer

Have each child take a turn saying this prayer:

Dear God, help me not to be happy when (name) gets in trouble,
instead let me help (name) learn to do nice things so that (name) won't get into trouble. Amen.

CLOUD GAZING

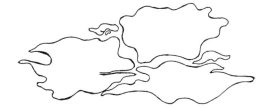

Materials Needed
- ✔ nice weather
- ✔ cumulous clouds (puffy)
- ✔ Bible

Setting the Stage

This is a devotional during which your imaginations can blossom. The purpose is to get your children thinking about Heaven. As you ask your questions don't be quick to say, "No!" to their answers. If an answer does need to be rethought, you can gently help them do so. For example, I am pretty sure there will be no drag car racing in Heaven, but we might be able to run fast through grassy fields. Only the last question has one right answer.

Project

Head out to a nearby park or favorite green space. Even your back yard will do. Lie together on the grass and look up into the clouds. While you are watching the clouds blow by, an adult needs to read *John 14:1-4.* After reading the verses ask your children the following questions. In between the questions leave plenty of time for the children to discuss, imagine and share their ideas.
- ✔ What are some things you hope will be in Heaven?
- ✔ What is the first thing you would like to do in Heaven?
- ✔ Do you see any shapes in the clouds that look like something you might find in Heaven? (possibilities: throne, angels, house or mansion)
- ✔ What is the most important thing we will be doing in Heaven? (praising God)

Song

Sing your favorite song that praises God (a little taste of what we will be doing in Heaven).

Prayer

You don't have to wait until you get to Heaven to praise God. You can do it here on earth. Choose one thing about God (patient, loving, helpful, kind) for which each of you is thankful. Say thank you to God for being that kind of God.

BOUQUET

Materials Needed
- ✔ two large, white poster boards per child
- ✔ markers or crayons
- ✔ scissors
- ✔ an outfit from each child's wardrobe
- ✔ a field of wild flowers
- ✔ Bible

Setting the Stage
After collecting the wild flowers and viewing their beauty your children will have the opportunity to make their own life size paper doll and dress it in their own clothes. It will be a time when your children can see how beautifully "dressed" the flowers of the field are and how God has provided good things for them as well.

Project
The flowers:
- ❀ Collect as many varied wild flowers as possible.
- ❀ Take the time to notice the colors and shapes.
- ❀ Bring the flowers home and together arrange a big bouquet for your table.

Our Clothes:
- ✂ Tape two poster boards together for each child.
- ✂ Have the children lie down on their board and trace their bodies, making sure to include the hair, hands and feet. Cut out the shape Note: The larger children might need to have their hands and feet taped on afterwards using leftover pieces of poster board.
- ✂ Allow your children to color the doll according to their own particular coloring and looks (blue eyes, curly hair).
- ✂ The children are to dress their dolls in their own clothes.
- ✂ When they see the end product, take time to let them see how well God has dressed them — just as God dresses the flowers.

Bible Reading Time:
Read *Matthew 6:25-30.* Let them tell you what the verses mean. The younger children will need to be asked some pointed questions.
- ♰ Who made the flowers?
- ♰ Did God make the flowers ugly or beautiful?
- ♰ From where do we get our clothes?
- ♰ How did we get the money to buy the clothes?
- ♰ Who gave us our jobs? (God did and God provides for us the same way he does for the birds and flowers).

Prayer
Thank God for the clothes, money and food we have, because we know it all comes from God.

NATURE COLLAGE

Materials Needed

- ✔ one white sheet of poster board
  (or one small piece of construction paper per child)
- ✔ glue
- ✔ a plastic bag per person

Setting the Stage

Nature itself is so varied, just like our God who created it. The purpose of this devotional is to find as many different items from nature as you can. Together take the time to enjoy the variety that reflects our God.

Project

Time to go back to nature:

- ✧ Bring the materials needed with you as you go to the nearest uncivilized area. Once you arrive let your children know you are going to make a picture about nature. They are to collect as many different items from nature as they can find. Note: They should be the type of items that can be glued to a piece of paper. Let them head off to collect. Each person should have a plastic bag in which to hold their findings. Give them 10 - 15 minutes to search for their varied treasures.

As you come back together:

- ✧ Find a spot where you can sit down, sort and organize the items. These pieces of nature can be sorted by color, size, type or texture. Once sorted, the adult will squeeze a drop of glue under each item as each person places this item from nature on the poster board. The fun part about a collage is that anything goes. The end product will doubtless be interesting, varied and in its own way beautiful.

Our God is also full of variety:

- ✧ See how many different details about God your children can share with you. Include a few of the details listed below.

patient	perfect	kind
loving	Father	Savior
gentle	friend	caring

Prayer

Have each person choose a favorite description of God. Then let each one tell God, "I think you are special because you are _____."

ROCK CRACKING

Materials Needed
- ✔ one large, relatively round rock (or hammer)
- ✔ one large, relatively flat rock (or hard flat surface)
- ✔ country road or rocky stream (where you can find lots of little and varied rocks)

Setting the Stage
We often judge people by first impressions, but it is really what is inside that is important to get to know. That is where the real beauty of a person can be seen. This is very true with rocks as well. As the children see this to be true with rocks, help them remember this important detail when they are meeting new people and making new friends.

Project
Location for this devotional is fairly important because you will want to be in a place where there are many different kinds of rocks from which to choose.

First:

Let each child choose five palm sized rocks. Ask them what they think the rock will look like inside. It really is a mystery most of the time because the inside does not always look like the outside. Take one rock at a time and start tapping it gently. Increase the strength of the tap until it finally cracks open. Note: If you start too hard you are bound to smash the rock and then it is difficult to see the real insides. Show the children the difference between the inside and the outside. Which is more beautiful? Usually it is the inside.

Next:

Discuss what it was like when each child met a friend for the first time. What were their first thoughts? If they do not remember, help them by telling them how they acted (shy, quiet, wondering the child's name or maybe not caring to talk to this new child). Now what do they think of their friend? Let them share about the friend and then show them that the details they are talking about have a lot more to do with the character of the friend (the inside) than with the friend's looks (the outside).

Finally:

Let your children try to explain to you where the real beauty of the rock is (inside). Then have your children tell you where the real beauty of people is (inside). Encourage them to look for the inner beauty in people and value that. Take the opportunity to show them this principle over the next week.

Prayer
Have the children ask God to help them value the inner beauty of other people. To help the children understand this you can mention specifics like, "Mary is so kind," or, "Joe can make you laugh." Take time now to talk to God about this.

GOD PROVIDES THROUGH GROWING THINGS

Materials Needed

✔ access to fruit (fruit stand, orchard, farm or grocery store)

✔ shish kabob sticks

✔ selection of favorite fruits (grapes, strawberries, bananas, mandarin orange sections, pineapple -anything that can easily be skewered with a stick)

Setting the Stage

The best food is what is grown naturally and is provided first hand by God. This is an opportunity to learn about this process and enjoy the "fruits" of your labor as well!

Project

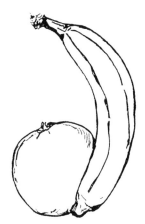

1. It would be best to visit a farm or an orchard first. Here you might have the chance to pick your own food (if it is that type of farm). If this is not readily available to you, the next best option is a fruit stand where the person selling the fruit can tell you a little about the product. Finally, if nothing else is available to you, it would still work to visit the fruit section of your grocery store. Share with your children yourown knowledge of how these items grow.

2. Allow the children to pick their favorite type of fruit to take home and eat. The fruit you pick for the shish kabobs needs to be firm and easily pierced.

3. When you get home let the children help wash the fruit. Cut up the fruit. Let the children make their own shish kabobs. Take the fruit sticks outside and go for a walk while you enjoy your tasty treat.

Prayer

This can be a fun kind of prayer (without being irreverent). Call out your thanks to God for the fruit as you are putting the pieces on your stick. For example, "Thank you God for a banana; thank you God for a grape; thank you God for an apple..."

COLORS IN NATURE

Materials Needed
✔ coloring book
✔ large selection of crayons
✔ colored candies (M&M's) or fruit salad
✔ favorite outdoor setting (woods or park)

Setting the Stage
God provides us with variety and beauty. As his children we need to learn to notice and appreciate that beauty. One way to do this is in nature itself. So as you wander through the woods or a park, take time to enjoy each other, notice the colors and say "thank you" to God.

Project

Instructions: Choose a favorite trail through the woods or a place in a park. Bring the coloring book, crayons andcolorful treats to eat. Enjoy your time on the walk, but also make it constructive by helping the children notice the different colors in nature.

Each time a new color is noticed:
☞ stop
☞ choose the closest color in your crayon selection that would match the color in the nature just seen
☞ let the child who noticed the color in nature fill in a portion of the chosen picture from the coloring book

The goal is to completely color the picture in the coloring book with the same colors that you saw in the out-of-doors while on your walk.

Treat Time (candies or fruit salad - can be either)
Choose either option:
◆ When a new color is found and recorded on the page in the coloring book, everyone gets the same color of treat to enjoy until the next color is identified.
◆ At the end, when the page in the coloring book is completely filled, stop and review the beauty of the colors and enjoy a colorful treat at the same time.

Song
"Jesus Loves the Little Children"
Jesus loves the little children, all the children of the world.
Red and yellow, black and white, they are precious in His sight.
Jesus loves the little children of the world.

When you are singing the colors, point to the colors that correspond on the page in the coloring book.

Prayer
Have everyone choose one of the colorful items they saw in nature and say "thank you" to God.

JESUS IS KING

Materials Needed

- ✔ cardboard (poster board or construction paper)
- ✔ foil (or crayons)
- ✔ masking tape (glue or stapler)
- ✔ bath towel
- ✔ safety pin
- ✔ timer

Setting the Stage

Jesus is the heavenly king who came to earth. He did this because he loved us so much. Yet, it must have been very hard for him to leave where he was loved as a king to come to earth where he was hated as a criminal. In this devotional the children will get a little feel for how hard it could have been.

Project

Making a Crown

✳ The best option is to take a piece of poster board or an empty cereal box and cut out a strip in the shape of a crown. The strip needs to be long enough to go around the child's head. Tape the strip together to form a circle and cover it with foil.

✳ The second option is to take a piece of construction paper and cut out a strip in the shape of a crown. The strip needs to be long enough to go around your child's head. Color with a crayon to make it look attractive. Glue, tape or staple the strip together to form a circle.

Establishing the Throne

✳ A chair should be set in the middle of the room and called the throne. The room itself is the throne room. Each child will have five minutes to be "king". Have this person put on the crown and attach the towel as a robe. During this time the "king" is allowed to tell everyone else in the throne room what to do. The guidelines are as follows:

*The king is a good king so he/she can only give kind orders.
*The orders can only be done in the throne room and may last only for the allotted time.
*Everyone must obey the orders!!

King for a time

❖ Establish the first king and set the timer for five minutes. As soon as you say "Go!" the king can start giving orders to one and all. You might need to give them some ideas on orders (jump, count to 20, sing a song, etc.). At the end of the five minutes the king will continue to give orders but no one will obey. Instead the rest are to laugh at the king. This laughing can go on for 20 - 30 seconds and then it is to stop.

❖ Ask the king how he/she felt when everyone was obeying. Then ask the king how he/she felt when everyone no longer obeyed but laughed instead.

❖ Repeat the process of becoming king and being questioned until all have had a turn.

How Jesus Must Have Felt

♦ Sit in a circle and take this time to point out to the children that Jesus experienced the same thing they just did, but he experienced it to a greater degree. Jesus was king in Heaven and everyone loved and obeyed him. Jesus chose to come to earth to die for us, because he loved us. It was still very hard for him to have people not obey him and laugh at him.

♦ Ask the children how Jesus must have felt during these times while he was here on earth.

♦ Next ask the children what would have made Jesus happy while he was here on earth.

♦ After they have answered, share with them that it is the same things that make Jesus happy now:

➠ loving him

➠ obeying him

➠ listening to his words (in the Bible)

➠ praying

Memory Verse

Luke 19:38

Blessed is the king who comes in the name of the Lord!

Ask the children...

Who is the king? (Jesus)

Where did this king go? (earth)

What does it mean, "In the name of the Lord"? (God wanted to send Jesus to earth)

Prayer

Ask God to help you to do those things that would make Jesus happy.

JESUS IS PERFECT

Materials Needed

✔ two puppets representing Jesus and Satan (you can substitute stuffed animals or dolls)
✔ table
✔ blanket
✔ construction paper
✔ scissors
✔ marker
✔ magazine
✔ glue

Setting the Stage

Beforehand read *Matthew 4:1-11*. During the devotional explain to the children that we are all tempted to do wrong things at one time or another. Jesus was tempted also, but he did not yield because he is perfect. We can learn from Jesus.

Project

 Puppet Show

Set up: Put your puppets and script behind a table that has been covered with a blanket. The blanket will give you privacy and make it look more like a puppet theater. Place Jesus on one hand and Satan on the other. Make sure your hands are raised high enough above the table top so the children, who are sitting in front of the blanket can see the puppets.

Note: You may use the Jesus puppet to introduce the Jesus section.

Jesus: (in the center of the stage) I have been here in the desert for 40 days praying to God. I am very hungry because I have not eaten anything for these 40 days.

Satan: I see that you are hungry, Jesus. Well, I know you can do anything so why don't you just turn those stones to bread and then you can eat them.

Jesus: Tempter, you know the Bible says, "Man does not live on bread alone, but on every word that comes from the mouth of God." That means that I did not move out here to the desert to eat but to pray and to listen to God, so stop tempting me to eat.

Satan: (moving to the right side of the table) Well, just come with me for a minute to this church. Let's go up to this high point on the church. We sure are up high. Hey, you are God, so why don't you jump down from here and let the angels catch you so you won't get hurt?

Jesus: Tempter, the Bible says, "Do not put the Lord your God to the test." I would be testing God by doing something like that and you know that I can't do that, so stop tempting me.

Satan: (moving to the left side of the table) Well, I just want to show you one more thing. Let's go up to the top of this mountain and take a look at the world. Sure is big. You know I have been put in charge of the world. That is why I am called the *Prince of this World.* If you bow down and worship me, I will give this whole world to you.

Jesus: Get away from me Tempter, for it is written in the Bible, "Worship the Lord your God, and serve Him only." You are not God and I would never worship you.

Satan: Well, I can't make you do anything wrong. Let's see, there must be someone else that I could tempt into doing something wrong. See you Jesus. (waves good-bye and drops behind the table)

Jesus: (turning to the children) The Tempter didn't get me to do anything wrong. One of the ways that I stopped him was by saying a Bible verse. That is why it's so important to learn

Let's try it right now:

♥ One of your friends tells you to lie to your mom so you won't get into trouble. What Bible verse should you say to your friend to let him/her know that you won't lie? (Wait for answer - if they get it right say "Super!" - if they get it wrong, make this suggestion " Do not lie".)

Here, take another try.

♥ Your mother wants you to clean your room but the little voice inside you says "No"! What verse should you say that will help you obey your mother? (Wait again for the answer— "Children obey your parents".)

Jesus: See, there are lots of verses that will help you learn to stop the Tempter from making you do something wrong. It would make me happy if you could learn to be more like me!! See you later. (Wave good-bye to the children and drop behind the table.)

Memory Verse

James 4:7b
Resist the devil, and he will flee from you.

Instructions:

1. Write the memory verse in large letters on a piece of construction paper. Leave a large blank spot for each of the following words: Resist, Devil and Flee.
2. Take a magazine and look for three pictures that best describe these three words. Cut out these pictures and glue them in the appropriate blanks on the construction paper.
3. Go over the verse together, showing the children how the pictures stand for words. Hang it on your fridge for the week and review the verse at meal times.

Magazine Picture Examples:

Resist—(not cooperating or arguing) child pushing something / stubborn looking person
Devil- (Satan, Tempter) angry 'evil' look on a face / black or dark color
Flee—(run away, leave) child running away / car driving away

Prayer

Have each person choose one area in which he / she is easily tempted. Then have everyone pray about this area, asking God to...

♥ help them learn to be more like Jesus.
♥ help them learn Bible verses so they can use a verse when they are being tempted to do some thing wrong.

JESUS IS OUR BEST FRIEND

Materials Needed
✔ one large piece of white paper (or eight sheets of white paper taped together)
✔ masking tape
✔ crayons or markers

Setting the Stage
After identifying the qualities of a best friend, you will look at how Jesus can be your best friend and how you can develop that relationship.

Project
Picture:

Place the large piece of paper on the wall at the children's eye level. Make sure it is in an area that is easily accessible to all. Sit around the paper in a semicircle so everyone has a good view of the paper.

1. First, draw a stick picture of a boy or girl.
2. Second, have the children describe for you the stick figure's best friend which is to be drawn beside it. At first they will tell you details about the outward appearance. Follow their instructions but help them to include details that will communicate a special friendship.
   These are some examples:
   ★ mouth in a smile (having fun together)
   ★ one hand holding the hand of the first child (friendship)
   ★ one hand holding out a toy for the first child (sharing)
   ★ clothes or something that is the same, for example, both are wearing a red top (enjoying the same things)
3. When you are finished the picture, point out what the picture communicates. Make sure you include some of the details mentioned in the brackets above.

Discussion:
The question to ask now is, "How can we make Jesus our best friend?". The answer is by spending time with him, getting to know him, and having fun talking to him (just as we do with our earthly friends).

Have them share some ideas about how you can practically do this. If they cannot come up with any ideas, choose one or two below:

☛ Read Bible stories in a children's Bible to get to know the things Jesus did.
☛ Pray to him during the day when you are playing or having some quiet time. Talk with him about the things you have been doing.
☛ Try to make Jesus happy in the way you act and then thank him for his help.

Sharing:
Choose one way each of you will try to get to know Jesus better this coming week (The adults should participate in the application part too!!). Share your choices with one another.

Prayer

Go around the circle thanking Jesus for wanting to be your best friend. Then go around the circle asking Jesus to help you carry out the choice you made earlier.

Song

"Jesus is My Friend"
(use the original tune or the tune of "One little Two little Three little Indians")
Jesus is my friend, Jesus is my friend, Jesus is my friend
and I'm so glad we're friends!

Learn the song together and then with your musical instruments stand up and march around the living room singing the song over and over again.

JESUS IS TO BE OBEYED

Materials Needed
none

Setting the Stage
Jesus gave us many commands and words of instruction while he was here on earth. During this devotional you will learn about a few of those commands, the importance of obeying them and the fact that Jesus made these rules because he loves us.

Project
First: A game of "Simon Says"
An adult will be Simon (at least for the first game). The rest of the group will stand in front of Simon. They all need to understand, before the game starts, that they are only to obey when Simon says, "Simon says!" An example of how the game can go:

☞ Adult says, "Simon says, 'Raise your arm'," -everyone raises their arm.

☞ Adult says, "Simon says, 'Turn around'," -everyone turns around (Note: If they lower their arm they are out because Simon did not say for them to lower their arm).

☞ Adult says, "Lower your arm." -everyone needs to remain perfectly still (if any one lowers their arm , they are out because the adult did not say "Simon says.")

You might need to give them a few trial runs because it takes a little while for the younger children to understand and remember. The goal of the game is to get all but one out. That person is the winner.

Second: Obeying Jesus
Sit in a circle and suggest some rules Jesus made while he was here on earth. Below are some suggestions if the list from the circle is a short one.

Matthew 5:21-22	We should not hate anyone.
Matthew 5:33-37	We need to do what we said we were going to do.
Matthew 5:42	We need to share and give to those who are in need.
Matthew 5:44	We should love our enemies and pray for those who are mean to us.

Third: How should we obey Jesus?
We should obey the same way we obeyed Simon, except we are to do only what "Jesus says"! We need to learn about and respond to all that Jesus wants us to do. Explain this to your children and emphasize that Jesus gave these commands because he loves us and wants the best for us.

Prayer
Choose one area each of you needs to work on so you can obey Jesus better. Everyone should take a turn asking God for help with that choice.

JESUS IS CARING

Materials Needed

✔ one sheet of white paper per child (or driveway)
✔ crayons (or sidewalk chalk)
✔ pen
✔ bowl
✔ slips of paper
✔ Bible

Setting the Stage

You do not have to look far to see the caring side of Jesus. This will be a time for your children to see this characteristic. As you read aloud the examples on the slips of paper, the children will have a chance to communicate the act of caring through their creative drawing.

An option is to allow them to draw on the driveway with sidewalk chalk rather than on a piece of paper with crayons (an added bonus could be that others in the neighborhood could also learn about the caring side of Jesus when you are doing this devotional outside).

Project

Write the following examples on slips of paper, fold them in half and place them in a bowl. Do this before the devotional begins.

✝ **John 19:26-27**: Even when Jesus was dying on the cross and in much pain, he still cared for his mother. When he saw her standing by the cross he made sure his friend would take care of her after he died.

✝ **John 11:1-5 & 11:32-44**: One of Jesus' best friends died. The man's name was Lazarus. Even though Jesus knew he was going to bring him back to life, Jesus still cried. This showed how much he cared for Lazarus and his two sisters.

✝ **Mark 10:13-16**: The parents wanted to have their children touched by Jesus. Jesus cared so much for the little children that when the men tried to stop the children from going to Jesus he responded, "Let the little children come to me!" The children came to Jesus and he blessed them.

✝ **Matthew 14:14**: Jesus spent a lot of time while he was on earth healing those who were sick. He helped a man walk who could not walk, a man see who could not see and a woman who was bleeding to stop bleeding. He did all this and more because he cared for the hurting people.

Share with the children that they are going to learn about how caring Jesus is. Allow each child to have a turn choosing a slip of paper from the bowl. After the adult reads the verse and what is written on the slip of paper all the children are to draw a little picture of what they just heard. Each picture will be a bit different. For the younger ones parents might have to draw the picture and let them color it. The end product will be either a page or a driveway filled with little pictures of how Jesus cared. Either way it will be a good reminder of how caring Jesus was and is.

Note: For the three to four year old choose one passage and one picture.

Memory Verse

I Peter 5:7b
He cares for you.

Ask your children how Jesus shows them that he cares. Some potential answers could be..."By giving us a warm home, loving parents, food to eat, nice friends, the Bible!!"

Prayer

Thank God that Jesus not only cared for people in the Bible, but that he also cares for us now.

JESUS IS OUR SAVIOR

Materials Needed

✔ small, beautifully wrapped box with slip of paper inside that reads, "Eternal Life - Heaven"
✔ plastic play food (or make your own play food with paper and crayons and a few cans from the cupboard)
✔ play money (or make your own play money with paper and crayons)

Setting the Stage

To help your children understand that a price had to be paid for us to get into Heaven, spend some time at a pretend grocery store. The whole issue really is that a price had to be paid for us to get into Heaven, but we could not pay the price...Jesus had to pay the price for us. Jesus in turn gave Heaven to us as a gift...we just need to say we are sorry for our sins and thank him for the gift.

Project

A mini grocery store needs to be established. Plastic or pretend food and money are the basics. The children get to go "shopping." When they are finished making their choices, you ask them to "pay the price" (using those exact words). When they cannot produce the money to "pay the price", one adult should bring out some pretend money and "pay the price" for them. After all the shopping is done, sit down and help them understand this principle: They wanted the groceries but couldn't "pay the price" so you paid it for them. People want to go to Heaven but they can't "pay the price" so Jesus paid it for them.
Ask them the following questions:

✎ Why did Jesus need to be the one paying the price? (Because he never sinned — he is perfect)
✎ What did Jesus do to pay the price? (He died on the cross)
✎ What does Jesus give to us? (The way to get to heaven if we accept the fact that he has paid the price for us).
✎ How do we accept the gift? (By saying sorry for our sins and thank you for the gift)

At this point bring out the previously wrapped gift. Hand it to your children but do not let go of the gift until the children say "Thank you" for it. Let the children open it and have the slip of paper read to them. Help the children make the connection with the gift they just received and the gift of eternal life Jesus offers to us. It is just as simple with Jesus' gift...we need to say thank you and make it our own.

Song

"Thank You Lord"
(use the original tune or "She'll be Coming Around the Mountain")
"Thank you Lord for saving my soul.
Thank you Lord for making me whole.
Thank you Lord for giving to me thy great salvation
so rich and free.

Memory Verse

John 3:16 (simplified)
God loved us so much that he gave Jesus to us, and whoever believes in Jesus will have eternal life.
(regular)
For God so loved the world that he gave his one and only son, that whoever believes in him shall not perish but have eternal life.

Prayer

Now would be a good time to say thank you to Jesus for dying on the cross, for paying the price and for giving us the gift of eternal life.

JESUS IS TO BE REMEMBERED

Materials Needed

✔ one small cup for each person
✔ one small plate
✔ a pitcher of grape drink
✔ a small piece of bread for each person
✔ pen, crayons or markers
✔ piece of plain white paper

Setting The Stage

In Luke 22:14-20 we see Jesus meeting with the disciples for the last time to have supper with them. It was during this meal that Jesus asked them to continue meeting together and to celebrate what we now call communion. Jesus was about to die. To symbolize his death, the drink was given to represent Jesus' blood that was to be spilt. The bread was given to represent Jesus' body that was to be broken.

There are two approaches that can be taken to help your children understand communion:

　　　a) Have the drink and bread laid out before them and explain to them what it means.
　　　b) Have a time for communion together, each taking the drink and bread.

If the children are old enough to have an understanding of what they are doing and if your church would not be alarmed by the act of a family taking communion together, it could be a very meaningful time for everyone.

Project

You can adapt this part so it fits with your choice of a) or b). Have a small amount of drink poured in each glass. Have the pieces of bread on a plate. Sit around a table with the bread and drink in the center of the table. At this point you can explain about the communion process or you can take communion together.

✳ Each person needs to take the time to say sorry to God for anything they have done wrong. This is called confessing your sins.
✳ An adult needs to thank God for dying on the cross and having his body hurt for us.
✳ As you pass around the pieces of bread, let each person take a piece and eat it. Explain to your children that they are to be thinking about how hurt Jesus' body must have been when he was on the cross and how thankful we need to be that he did this for us.
✳ As you pass out each cup, again explain to your children that they are to be thinking about the fact that Jesus' blood was poured on the ground and then he died.
✳ While he was on the cross he went through all of this for us.

Memory Verse

Luke 22:19b
Do this in remembrance of me.

This can be done in a dot to dot form. Do the writing of the verse in dots beforehand. Let the children rotate doing one word at a time as the verse appears before them. Place the verse on the fridge to review at mealtimes during the coming week.

Prayer

End your time together by having each person take a turn to say thank you to Jesus.

JESUS IS ALWAYS WITH US

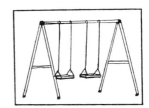

Materials Needed
✔ Bible
✔ one sheet of paper per child
✔ crayons
✔ thumb tack or masking tape

Setting The Stage
How can you know that Jesus is near if you can't see him? This is a hard concept for anyone to really accept, but it is true and it is what you will want your children to understand a bit better once this devotional is finished.

Project
Read to your children Hebrews 13:5b. The part of the verse you are to read is, "Never will I leave you," but let them see that you are reading it from the Bible. Tell them this is a promise in the Bible that we have to believe is true even if we can't see Jesus.

Ask them when they most need to have Jesus with them. Their answer needs to be in a situation they can visualize because they will be drawing it later.

Some ideas would be:
○ playing in the back yard with Billy
○ beside my desk at school
○ when I go to sleep at night

Draw a picture of the situation they just described. Each person is to draw his/her own suggestion. Younger children will need your help because you want the picture to be recognizable.   God can be put into the picture as a yellow light or a space where he would be.

Take the completed pictures to the bedrooms and have each child tack his/her picture up beside his/her bed. Before they go to bed at night and when they wake up in the morning, they will see their picture and be reminded that Jesus is always with them.

Memory Verse
Hebrews 13:5b
Never will I leave you

Prayer
Thank Jesus for being with us always even when we can't see or feel him.

BIBLE STORIES IN A ROUND

Materials Needed
✔ your imagination

Setting the Stage
This is an opportunity for you to review creatively with your children the stories you have learned from the Bible. The main facts should remain correct and in order, but allow the children to add their own creative flair as they tell their part.

Project
Instructions: Pick a Bible story and take turns telling the story by going around in a circle using one or two sentences each. Try to have an adult begin and end the story. As you go around the circle each person should take a turn at least once. Everyone should finish their turn by saying, "Next." An example has been provided below.

Daniel and the Lion's Den

Adult: Daniel was a man who loved God. He showed this by praying to God three times every day. Next.

Child: Some bad men didn't like him praying to his God. Next.

Adult: The bad men went to the king and asked the king to make a law so the people in the land would pray only to the king and no other gods. Next.

Child: The king made the law. The bad men went to watch and see if Daniel was still going to pray to his God. Next.

Child: Daniel loved God and so he still got down on his knees and prayed to God three times a day. The bad men saw him doing this. Next.

Adult: The bad men went to the king and told him that Daniel was still praying to his God. So the king had to throw Daniel into the lion's den, and that made the king very sad because he liked Daniel. Next.

Child: Daniel got thrown into the lion's den but he prayed that the lions wouldn't eat him, and the lions didn't. Next.

Adult: It was God who shut the mouths of the lions. Next.

Child: The king called to Daniel and asked if he was okay. Daniel said that the lions hadn't eaten him. Next.

Child: So the king took Daniel out and threw the bad men into the lion's den, and the lions ate them all up. Next.

Adult: The king made it a law that everyone in the land should pray to Daniel's God, and that made Daniel very happy.

Prayer
This would be a good opportunity to have a little prayer to end the story. This does not have to happen each time but it does fit well with the story of Daniel and the Lion's Den.

GOD'S CHARACTER

Materials Needed
✔ A Sunday school song book (optional)

Setting the Stage
There are many descriptive words for God found in the songs we sing to him. To help pass the time in the car, this activity will get you thinking as well as having a lot of fun.

Project
This car devotional is a game that is approachable from two different directions.
First:
- ❂ You go around the circle in the car and each person takes a turn.
- ❂ The first person calls out this phrase, "God is _____ ." It is his/her choice what word is put in the blank.
- ❂ The first person in the car to come up with a Sunday school song that has the same word in it will get one point.
- ❂ The person who suggested the word has to wait thirty seconds before answering with a song title.
- ❂ Once a song is given, you take a break in the game to sing the song together.

This is a great game for children who are a little older. Of course, the person with the most points at the end wins. To help finish the game a predetermined winning number can be established. For example the first one to reach five points wins. This game will help the children not only think of new and different characteristics of God, but it will also give them a chance to sing their favorite songs to God.

Second:
- ❇ The second option is a better one for the younger children in the car. It is a challenge between the little ones and the big ones.
- ❇ The children will have the sole responsibility to call out this phrase, "God is _____ ." They are to fill in the blank with a descriptive word about God.
- ❇ Once the phrase has been said, the adults in the car have to come up with a Sunday school song that everyone knows and that also has the chosen word in the lyrics.
- ❇ Once the title of the song is given, everyone takes the time to sing the song together. The object of the game is to stump the adults. The first child to do so gets a big cheer!!

To help you get on the way with this game you will find a few ideas below. Happy singing!!
God is...LIGHT = "This Little Light of Mine"
God is...LOVE = "Jesus Loves Me"
God is...GOOD = "God is so Good"

Song
Once you are finished playing the game, continue singing the same songs all over again.

GOD IN NATURE

Materials Needed

Setting the Stage

As we travel in the car we pass by many things our God has made. This devotional helps us to take notice of these things and also gives us a chance to say thank you to God for his creation.

Project

Allow a time span of five minutes to look out the car windows. During this time notice and call out all the things that are a part of God's creation. Note: If the children mention human made objects, help them understand that God made the material and people made the structure.

When the five minutes are up, the adult will choose any color and call it out. The children must then list off the previously mentioned items that fall under this color category. Continue this until all the colors have been mentioned.

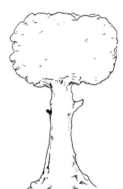

     Example: Green - grass
                 - leaves
                 - weeds
                 - moss
                 - reeds

When you are finished categorizing the items by color, have the children tell you the colors that did not have an answer (probably colors like purple or orange). Take the next five minutes for everyone to look out the window until a part of God's creation, in that particular color, is found.

Prayer

Allow each person to say this simple prayer, "Thank you God for making the _____." Have each person fill in the blank with one of the items from God's creation that was mentioned earlier.

SING-A-LONG

Materials Needed
✔ Sunday school song book (optional)

Setting the Stage
Music can calm the savage beast and can also do a lot for children who are getting restless in a car. This is a time to soothe, relax and calm the children and yourselves. Spend the time worshipping God as well as reviewing old favorites and learning new treasures.

Project
It is as simple as singing...
> You can trust your memory and go for it.
> You can get a church song book and use it.
> You can make a list of favorites and leave it in the car.
> You can buy a children's sing-a-long tape to use in the car.
> You can pick and choose some from the following list.

Here is a list of some of the best loved Sunday school songs (add your favorites to it).

Deep and Wide
Give Me Oil in my Lamp
God is so Good
Hallelujah, Praise Ye the Lord
He is Lord
Heavenly Sunshine
I Have the Joy
I Will Make You Fishers of Men
Jesus Loves Me
Jesus Loves the Little Children
My God is so Big
My God is an Awesome God
Peace like a River
What a Friend We Have in Jesus
Thank You Lord
This is the Day
This Little Light of Mine

TWENTY QUESTIONS

Materials Needed

Setting the Stage

This is a great game to help your children remember Bible characters. It will work best if everyone stays within the scope of familiar characters. You will be amazed at their ability once you have completed the Old Testament Story section in this book.

Project

The way to play:

You can go from youngest to oldest and give everyone a chance to "think."

- The first person to take a turn will think of a Bible character without saying who it is.
- The rest of the people in the car can take turns asking yes/no questions.
- The group as a whole is allowed 20 questions to figure out the character.
- As soon as someone thinks they know, they can call out the name, but they need to remember if it is wrong they have used up one of their 20 questions.

The more you play the game the more skilled the children will become at asking appropriate questions. The first few times you play this game the adults will have to take the lead, give some examples and be willing to be flexible until everyone knows what is happening.

An Example:

1. Is it a girl? no
2. Is it a lady? no
3. Is it a boy? yes
4. Is he nice? yes
5. Do we see him when he is all grown up? yes
6. Is he in the Old Testament? yes
7. Is he known for helping somebody? no
8. Did he write a book in the Bible? yes
9. Did he kill somebody? yes
10. Did he kill a giant? yes
11. Is it David? yes!!

You will find a lot of time can pass playing this game while you are on those long trips. It is also good for those short trips when the kids are going wild.

EASTER

Note: Some work must be done the day before

Materials Needed

- ✔ half a piece of poster board or a back section from a large empty cereal box
- ✔ half a cup of flour and half a cup of water mixed together in a bowl
- ✔ empty cardboard juice can and lid
- ✔ newspaper
- ✔ two popsicle sticks
- ✔ a fair amount of brown and green paint
- ✔ green, red and yellow construction paper
- ✔ glue
- ✔ paint brushes
- ✔ sponge
- ✔ one white sheet of paper
- ✔ crayons
- ✔ tape
- ✔ children's Bible (optional)

Setting the Stage

This devotional is really two in one. The first stage is putting together the paper mache Calvary and grave. After a day of drying, the scene will be ready for painting and decorating. While this decorating is taking place the salvation story can be told. Once the decoration is completed, it is the children's turn to tell the special story to you. It's a story that can change their lives!

Project

Note: This is a devotional for older children. If you feel your children are still too young to benefit from this format, take the time to tell the Easter story as found in Part III of this devotional. This may happen at the dinner table while you are enjoying your Easter dinner.

I. Paper Mache

Mount Calvary and the Grave: Rip two sheets of newspaper into 2" x 8" strips. Mix together the flour and water. Lay the piece of cardboard in front of you; take half a sheet of newspaper and wad it up into a ball. Set the ball in the center of the cardboard. This is to be Mount Calvary. Next, you need to cut the top three-fourths off of the juice can leaving only the bottom and one inch of the sides. Lay the juice can on its side, resting on the cardboard. Tape the juice can to the edge of the paper ball so the mouth of the can opens to the front of your display. This is the grave.

Run the strips through the flour and water mixture making sure they are completely wet. Then run the strip through your fingers removing the excess mixture. Lay the strips over the ball and tin and onto the cardboard forming the gentle slope of a hill. Overlap the strips at different angles and in a nonuniform design until the ball and tin are effectively covered. The end result should look like a cave that has been cut out of a rock. Paper mache the lid on all sides. This is the stone for the tomb.

Allow these to dry for about 24 hours so they are easily painted. A blow dryer can help rush this process if needed.

II. Decoration

a. Painting: The cardboard and hill are painted green. The fastest and easiest way is to dip the sponge into the green paint and let the children dab it all over the appropriate area. The tomb and stone are painted brown with a brush.

b. The Garden: The tomb Jesus was buried in was in a garden so we need to add a few trees and some flowers. The trees are made out of one popsicle stick broken in half and green construction paper for the leaves. The flowers are made from the colored construction paper to create a beautiful garden. Poke small holes into the cardboard where the trees are to stand (on either side of the tomb). Put glue around the base of the popsicle sticks. The trees will need to be held in place until the glue dries. The flowers are glued onto the cardboard.

c. The Cross: The second popsicle stick needs to be broken at the one-third/two-thirds mark. This will enable the two-thirds part to be the vertical long piece and the one-third part to be the horizontal cross piece. Glue these two pieces together to form a cross and hold in place until the glue is dry. Poke a hole in the top of your paper mache hill and stick the base of the cross into the hole. Put a little glue around the base to help hold it in place.

d. Jesus: A small paper doll figure of a man needs to be cut from the sheet of paper. Dark hair, a face with a beard and clothes need to be drawn on our Jesus. Although we do not really know what he looked like, we can try to imagine.

III. The Story:

You need to tell the details of Jesus' crucifixion and resurrection to your children while you are doing the decorating. This can be done by reading the story from a children's Bible or you can tell the story in your own words. The story is found in Luke 22-24.

Make sure the details below are included in the telling of this special story.

- ♱ Jesus was arrested, tried and found guilty. These bad people sentenced Jesus to death on a cross.
- ♱ Jesus was perfect, which means he had never done anything wrong, so these bad people were wrong in what they were doing.
- ♱ These bad people beat Jesus, spit on him and laughed at him.
- ♱ Then they took Jesus and nailed him to the cross where he died.
- ♱ Jesus' friends took his body, wrapped it in cloth and placed him in a nearby grave.
- ♱ The bad people wanted to make sure that he stayed in the grave so they rolled the stone over the front of the grave and put guards in front of the tomb to keep anyone from opening the grave.
- ♱ Three days later Jesus was brought back to life. God moved the stone to let Jesus out.
- ♱ The guards were so surprised they fainted.
- ♱ Jesus was alive again and he showed himself to his friends.
- ♱ Jesus stayed a bit longer on earth and then in a flash he went back up to Heaven.

IV. The Retelling

Now it is the children's turn to tell the story using the paper doll figure. Help them to incorporate into their story as many details as possible from what you told them earlier. During the Easter holiday let your children tell the story over and over. It would even be good to use your Calvary and Garden Tomb display as a centerpiece for the Easter dinner so the story can again be shared with those around the table.

<u>Prayer</u>

Not only do you want your children to understand the details of the story, but also the fact that Jesus suffered and died for us. As you study Jesus in the *Getting to Know Jesus* section, the whole plan of salvation will be understood better by your children, but right now you want them to take time to say thank you to Jesus for going through all of this for us, because it is through Jesus' death that we have eternal life.

MAY DAY

Materials Needed

- ✔ watermelon
- ✔ lemonade
- ✔ small ball
- ✔ bucket
- ✔ outdoor furniture for an obstacle race

Setting the Stage

There are many examples of people in the Bible who loved to celebrate. They celebrated for many reasons.

- 📖 *II Samuel 6:12-16* - King David celebrates the return of the ark.
- 📖 *Luke 15:17-24* - A father celebrates a son who comes back home.
- 📖 *John 2:1-10* - Jesus and his disciples are celebrating a wedding.

We too have many reasons to celebrate and today's devotional will help us celebrate Spring!! This devotional can be done in your back yard. It is best to wait for a day when the weather is wonderful!

Project

Talk about the reasons people celebrated in the Bible. Some reasons are listed above. Let the children know that you are about to celebrate Spring. A May Day celebration is filled with fun, games and food. You can be as elaborate or as simple as you like. A few ideas are provided. You may wish to invite guests to join in this celebration.

Who Made Spring?

Start off the celebration by asking who made the Spring. Ask the question a few times until they enthusiastically call out, "God." Take time to thank God for Spring and a chance to celebrate together. Then let the festivities begin.

The Games

- ○ Ring Around the Rosy: Everyone joins hands and sings the song, falling down at the end of the song (this might be reserved for children only).
- ○ London Bridge is Falling Down: Two children (or adults) hold hands raising them above their heads to form an archway. The other children (and adults) go under the "bridge" of arms while everyone sings... "London bridge is falling down, falling down, falling down. London bridge is falling down, my fair lady." On the word "lady" the bridge falls down catching someone in-between. This can be played over and over again.
- ○ Ball toss: A bucket is set two feet from the child and the child is given a ball. The child is to toss the ball into the bucket. Each time they make it, move the bucket a little further away. Make sure, though, that the child ends with success rather than frustration.
- ○ Obstacle course: Using readily available backyard pieces, set up your own obstacle course. There should be things to run around, climb over and climb under. Have a starting and finishing point. For the older children you can make it a bit of a competition by timing them. The younger children need to be cheered just for finishing the course.
- ○ Hide-and-go-seek
- ○ Tag
- ○ Other favorites

The Food!!

The menu can simply be watermelon and lemonade or as complicated as a full-fledged picnic dinner. Keep it to food that you associate with picnics and spring.

The Finish

A nice way to end your time of celebrating would be to go for a family walk.

Prayer

As you walk think of things that have been fun about your celebrating time. Thank God that he is a God who loves to celebrate.

CARD FOR A KING (FATHER'S DAY)

Materials Needed

✔ one piece of construction paper for each child
✔ one piece of white paper for each child
✔ crayons or markers
✔ salt
✔ yellow food coloring
✔ glue
✔ scissors

Setting the Stage

This devotional will give the children an opportunity to make a card for their Heavenly Father. Follow the basic plan but allow your child's own personality to come through in what he/she creates.

Project

1. Take a piece of construction paper and fold it in half.
2. Cut the piece of white paper in half and trim the edges so that one inch of construction paper will be seen when the white piece of paper is glued to the inside of the card.
3. Glue the white paper to the inside bottom half of the card.
4. Decorate the front of the card with a picture that communicates your child's view of God.
   Examples:
   Crown for a King: Adult draws a crown shape out of glue
   Child sprinkles colored salt* onto the glue, shakes off the excess and allows the glue to dry.
   Throne: Adult draws a throne shape out of glue. Child sprinkles colored salt* onto the glue, shakes off the excess and allows glue to dry.
   Caring Father: Draw a picture of God holding children on his lap.
   Friends: Draw a picture of God and a child walking through a park, holding hands and talking.

5. Inside the card, on the white piece of paper, write the message your children want to say to God. Help direct them to an attitude of thankfulness for what God has done for them.

* Make the colored salt by adding a few drops of yellow food coloring to the salt and mixing it together in a bowl or pan. Microwave or bake the salt until dry (two minutes for microwave or ten minutes at 350°F for oven).

Prayer

When all the cards are finished, come together as a family and present your cards to God. Have each person take time to read their message to God and say thank you for being such a wonderful Heavenly Father.

Memory Verse

Matthew 6:9b

Our Father in heaven, hallowed be your name.

For younger children:

Our Father in heaven, may your holy name be honored.

THANKSGIVING

Materials needed

✔ one piece of colored construction paper per person
✔ one sheet of white paper per person
✔ glue
✔ crayons
✔ masking tape
✔ magazines (optional)
✔ scissors (optional)

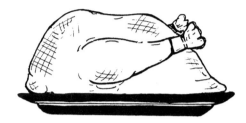

Setting the Stage

The focus of our Thanksgiving meal should be on those things for which we are truly thankful. To prepare everyone, do this devotional ahead of time and display the artwork on the walls around the table where the Thanksgiving meal will be celebrated.

Project

✔ Make a list of what everyone is thankful for this year. Help the children think over the year and maybe choose something that is not as obvious as "my parents." Everyone needs to choose the one thing they would like to draw. Each person in the family, even the adults, needs to do this because it can be used later at the mealtime.

✔ The picture is drawn on the white sheet of paper. If the younger children are not able to communicate their thoughts very well through pictures, you can let them look through a magazine and find a picture that says it for them. Cut the picture out of the magazine and glue it onto the white sheet.

✔ Once the artwork is completed, take the white sheet and glue it onto the colored construction sheet of their choice. Take the finished product and tape it on the wall that is near the Thanksgiving table.

Prayer

During the meal review each picture and let the individual artist have a chance to thank God for that particular thing.

CHRISTMAS

Materials Needed
✔ basket or decorated box
✔ small gift items
✔ tissue paper
✔ bow

Setting the Stage

God gave us his son Jesus as a gift. Jesus came as a little baby and it is the birth of Jesus and the giving of that gift that we are celebrating at Christmas. To help instill in your children the idea of giving, you will be making gift boxes to distribute to others to help make this season a special one for them.

Project

This devotional is one that can be shared with so many and changed a bit from year to year. It has become a family tradition in our home, and we have fun planning what we are going to do for others each Christmas season.

There are a few guidelines that should remain the same...
- ❏ The boxes or baskets should be a family effort. Everyone should be involved in the making and distributing of them.
- ❏ As you approach the door to give the chosen people their gift, greet them first with a Christmas carol that all can sing (they will love it whether you are on tune or not).
- ❏ Choose people you will not be giving a gift to at Christmas.

Here is where you can vary it and have some fun...
- ❏ The items in the box can be on a particular theme or a variety of items you know they would enjoy. It can be baked goods, homemade items, creams and bath salts, candy, games and so on.
- ❏ The box can be decorated with wrapping paper or brown paper which your children can decorate with drawings.
- ❏ The people can vary each year or remain the same. It is a good gift to give to older people or others who have served you over the past year (pastor, Sunday school teacher, sports coach, etc.)

Finishing touches...

Place the tissue paper in the bottom of the box or basket. Fill the box with the items you have chosen or made and place a bow on top.

It will be a fun and enjoyable evening spent delivering these gifts with your love and best wishes!

Prayer

As you are walking or driving to the next house for delivery, take time to say a prayer for that person or family. The prayer can have two aspects. The first is one of thanksgiving for the role they have played in your lives. The second is one of blessing for them for the coming year.